W9-ABI-867

How to Interview Like A Pro

Forty-Three Rules for Getting Your Next Job

MARY GREENWOOD
JD, LLM

National Science Foundation Library

iUniverse, Inc.
Bloomington

HF
5549.5
.I6
G744
2012

How to Interview Like A Pro
Forty-Three Rules for Getting Your Next Job

Copyright © 2010, 2012 Mary Greenwood, JD, LLM

All rights reserved. No part of this book may be used or reproduced by any means, graphic, electronic, or mechanical, including photocopying, recording, taping or by any information storage retrieval system without the written permission of the publisher except in the case of brief quotations embodied in critical articles and reviews.

iUniverse Star
an iUniverse, Inc. imprint

iUniverse books may be ordered through booksellers or by contacting:

iUniverse
1663 Liberty Drive
Bloomington, IN 47403
www.iuniverse.com
1-800-Authors (1-800-288-4677)

Because of the dynamic nature of the Internet, any Web addresses or links contained in this book may have changed since publication and may no longer be valid. The views expressed in this work are solely those of the author and do not necessarily reflect the views of the publisher, and the publisher hereby disclaims any responsibility for them.

ISBN: 978-1-938908-06-4 (pbk)
ISBN: 978-1-938908-07-1 (ebk)

Library of Congress Control Number: 2012912078

Printed in the United States of America

iUniverse rev. date: 7/19/2012

To Jack and Peggy Greenwood,
my wonderful parents, *in memoriam*

Contents

Acknowledgments

I want to thank my mom and dad, who instilled a love of words and literature in me at a very young age. They were always a source of great encouragement for me and my sisters.

I want to thank my son, John, an attorney and mediator, for giving me some good ideas about interviewing and sharing some anecdotes with me.

I also want to thank everyone who has ever interviewed me, whether I got the job or not. Those experiences, good and bad, inspired me to write this book.

Preface

This is the third in my series of books that started with *How to Negotiate Like a Pro:41 Rules for Resolving Disputes*, which is in its second edition and has won eight book awards. Next came *How to Mediate Like a Pro:42 Rules for Mediating Disputes*, which has won twelve book awards and so far *How to Interview Like a Pro: 43 Rules for Getting Your Next Job* has won twelve book awards, including the winner of the Indie Excellence Awards in the Career category, Winner of the Reader Views Book Awards in the How To category and the Silver Award Winner of the ForeWord Book Awards in the Career category.

My sister Sara suggested that I write a book about interviewing , since everyone entering the workplace—especially in this downward economy—could use a book on interviewing and how to get a job. Then it hit me that interviewing with a prospective employer is really a type of negotiation. If the employer makes a job offer, then the negotiation continues as benefits and salary are determined. It seemed a logical sequence to call the third book in the series *How to Interview Like a Pro: 43 Rules for Getting Your Next Job.*

A few years ago, I wrote a book for employers called *Hiring, Firing, and Supervising Employees: An Employer's Guide to Discrimination Laws*, but I have always wanted to write a book for applicants and employees. I have been an employment and labor attorney for over twenty-five years and know the laws of hiring and interviewing. I have worked as a human resources director for over ten years and interviewed for a search firm for over five years. I also know about interviewing from my own career. At last count, I have held over twenty-five different jobs, and that translates into hundreds of job interviews. I include some practical anecdotes from my own experiences.

How to Interview Like a Pro: 43 Rules for Getting Your Next Job will give you strategies and practical tips about the interview process. It will give you insight into how get ready for an interview, how to answer those difficult questions, and how to negotiate salary. It will also help you understand the laws of interviewing and the questions an employer cannot legally ask you. There are reference materials in the appendices, including a glossary of terms, a list of state and federal resources, and the dos and don'ts of interviewing. After you read this book, you should be able to interview like a pro.

Introduction

Getting a job is like parking.
You have to be at the right place at the right time.

Just like most things in life, timing is very important. You have to be at the right place at the right time. One thing that is always interesting about the interview process is that you really don't know what is happening on the other side of the interview. You don't know where the company is in the interview process or what they are really looking for. This book will give you some tips and advice so that when your opportunity comes, you will be ready during each step of the process.

Once, when looking for a job, I took a map (this is before Google and GPS systems) and used a protractor to arc the distance from my new apartment to see what towns were nearby. I saw that if I went over the Sunshine Skyway Bridge, a neighboring city was only ten miles away. I picked up my briefcase with resumes, got dressed for a job interview, and drove over that bridge. I found out that the county administrator was looking for an attorney. I knocked on his door and introduced myself. The county administrator looked at me as though he could not believe his good luck; he read my resume and interviewed me on the spot. It turned out the county administrator had already advertised for the position, did not like any of the candidates, and was getting pressure to hire someone quickly. He asked me to come back, and I started my new job within the week.

That was when I first realized that getting a job was like parking. Was I the best candidate? Probably not, but I did have experience. I was available, and I was there. It is amazing what a protractor can do. My point is to get out there so that when somebody pulls out of his or her parking spot, you are ready to drive into that spot and get the job.

Chapter 1.

HOW TO
GET STARTED

Rule 1. Getting a Job is a full-time job.

If you already have a job and are looking for another job, then you have two full-time jobs. Getting a job is not for the faint of heart. If you do not currently have a job, this is not the time to sleep late, read the paper, and smell the roses. This is the time to get up early, get dressed in office clothes, and start looking for a job. Your computer is probably going to be your steady companion. Check certain websites on a regular basis and submit résumés. However, you are not going to get a job just sitting at your computer; you have to get out and about as well. Make contacts daily, and make luncheon plans with people who can help you.

Getting a job is hard work. You don't just send out your résumé and wait for a response. You apply for a lot of jobs simultaneously. You write a polished résumé. You make sure that everything you send out is well written and has no typos. You act as though this is serious business, which it is. Since this is your job, you should be spending eight hours or more each day looking for a job. There will be times when you get discouraged, but you have to pick yourself up and start all over again.

Rule 2. Prepare a good elevator speech.

An elevator speech is a short speech that you could give on an elevator ride that tells in thirty seconds or less who you are, what you can offer, and what you can bring to the job. You should give just enough information so that you can finish your speech by the time the elevator door opens, and you should leave that person in the elevator wanting to ask you some questions. If that person gets back into the elevator, you will know you made an impression.

This is your pitch. You can use your elevator speech in job interviews, at job fairs, and in chance encounters with friends or strangers. Wherever you are, you should be talking to someone about your job prospects.

Here is one of my elevator speeches: "My name is Mary Greenwood. I am a labor attorney and human resource director who has written three award-winning books, one on negotiations, one on mediation, and one on interviewing. My greatest strength is conflict resolution, and I want to work as a mediator or ombudsman." You can tweak it for each occasion or have two versions; I have one for conflict resolution and one for teaching. Here's the teaching version: "My name is Mary Greenwood and I have over ten years experience teaching employment discrimination, labor law, and alternate dispute resolution. In addition, I have written three award-winning books on negotiations, mediation and interviewing. I thoroughly enjoy teaching and would like to get back into higher education."

Rule 3. Make a list of everyone you know.

Think of all the people you know and write down their addresses, including e-mail addresses and telephone numbers. Get out your rolodex (some people still have them), your cell phone contacts, your stack of business cards, and your e-mail list to make your list complete. Think of all your childhood, high school, and college friends. They don't have to be your peers or the same age. Friends' parents can be very valuable because they already have jobs and may even be in a position to hire you themselves. Think of people in your church, at your jazzercise class, or at your hair salon. You are getting the idea. As you write their names down, think of where they work now and where they have worked in the past. Don't forget all your relatives. You may get an aha moment even as you are writing the list. "I forgot that Aunt Suzie is a head hunter. I wonder if she remembers me." Go back to this list and keep expanding it. People generally like to help people, especially friends or relatives, if given the opportunity. They may even know about a position before it is advertised.

Rule 4. Tell everyone you know you are looking for a job.

Contact everyone on the list and tell them your elevator speech. Even if your contacts do not know of any job openings, they may keep you in mind if they hear about something opening up. Call or e-mail them and then follow up with a copy of your résumé. Explain what type of position you are seeking and see if any of these contacts know of anyone in the field who might be able to help you. Even if your contact does not know of a position, he or she may be able to give you some advice about working for his or her company or what types of positions might become available at a later time.

In addition, these people can be a wonderful resource for you. They may have some advice to help you get your foot in the door. Ask to visit their workplaces so you can look around and be introduced. Don't forget to tell everyone you see. When you are on the phone, say, "By the way, I have been laid off and am looking for a job in human resources. Do you know anyone who works in that field?" Even if you don't believe that your doctor or dentist is going to help you find a job, tell him anyway. The conventional wisdom is that many jobs are not posted. You may find out about something that hasn't even been posted. Everyone has been in the position of not having a job, and most remember what it is like. Have some business cards made up so people will know how to get in touch with you.

Rule 5. Tell everyone you would like to know you are looking for a job.

Social networking has changed the way we socialize both at work and in our private lives. We can find someone with similar interests anywhere in the world. One networking site I particularly like is LinkedIn (www.linkedin.com). It has been called the Facebook for adult professionals. The philosophy is basically this: the people you know also know other people worth knowing. After you sign up, you can find out who on your e-mail list is already a member of LinkedIn. This is a way to let people know you need a job, and you can join groups in your field of interest. For example, I have joined such diverse groups as mediators, alternate dispute resolution professionals, human resources professionals, dog lovers, and alumni groups. You will also be able to find former colleagues in all the jobs that you have previously held.

The idea is to keep expanding your network. You can send messages and make comments in discussion groups. It is a good way to make contacts and find out about job openings. Let it be known that you are looking for a job and join groups that specialize in looking for a job. While online networking is a useful tool, I don't think networking in person will ever be completely replaced. There is something to be said about communicating face to face. If you are trying to get a position in the area where you live, try to meet up with professionals in your field or the field you want to work in. Join a local professional group in your field and participate in meetings. You might also want to volunteer to speak in your field so you can get known.

Rule 6. Prepare a great résumé.

You must write a résumé that summarizes your job experience, education, skills, and accomplishments. Someone reading résumés makes a judgment about yours in a few seconds. You want to make those few seconds count so your future employer will take a second look. Any spelling errors or other quirks will immediately stand out and be a reason for rejection even before a potential employer gets to your qualifications for the job. Although I always prepare a cover letter with my résumé (see rule number 7 below), I assume that the cover letter may somehow get separated from the résumé. Therefore, I try to make sure that the résumé can stand alone. I usually put my objective at the top of the first page so it is clear what type of job I am seeking. When I am applying to a specific company, I will write that company's name as well: "My objective is to find a senior level human resources position at Company A." Sometimes I will put a short summary of my experience at the top of the résumé, again with the thought that the cover letter might not be read or even be available.

Rule 7. Prepare a great cover letter.

I always do a cover letter, because I believe that the cover letter is really more important than the résumé itself. It may be tempting not to bother with a cover letter, especially when sending the résumé electronically. However, if you send a résumé without a cover letter, you are doing yourself a big disservice. A cover letter is a good opportunity for you to go beyond your résumé and highlight the specific experience you have that correlates with the requirements of the position. A well-written cover letter can make your qualifications stand out. I like to go over each requirement of the job listing and spell out the experience I have in that area. I also try to explain in my cover letter why I am uniquely qualified for this position and why I think I am the best candidate.

Rule 8. Be in interview mode all the time.

When you are looking for a job, remember that you have to be in interview mode at all times. First impressions are very important. For example, when you pick up an application, you need to look professional, not as though you just got out of bed. An employer told me about an applicant who wore bedroom slippers and short shorts while picking up an application. Often the person you get the application from is the same person who will interview you. If you are wearing bedroom slippers and shorts, the employer does not need to read the application to decide you are not employee material. Any conversation with anyone at a prospective employer is a potential interview. How you treat the receptionist or an employee on the phone is as important as making an impression on the boss. If someone is rude to you, it may be a test to see how you react. If someone in the interview chain has a negative impression of you because of something you said, most likely the person making the final decision will hear about it.

Rule 9. Be flexible.

You have to be flexible. For example, you should be willing to meet for an interview at a nontraditional location. If an interviewer wants to meet you at a chamber of commerce meeting or a marketing firm invites you to go to a presentation to a client, you should go. There is probably a good reason behind the chosen meeting spot. For one thing, it could be more convenient for the interviewer. It could be a test to see if you are actually dedicated to your field. It could also be a test of your networking and social skills. My son was asking a candidate to meet him for lunch to discuss a position in his law firm. The candidate said he did not have time for lunch because he was looking for a job. Somehow he did not get the notion that this was part of the interview process. When questioned about whether he was really looking for a job, he responded that he thought my son wanted to discuss the law in general. Needless to say, he did not get the job.

Of course, in the interest of safety, you are not going to meet in a dark alley or other dangerous place.

Chapter 2. How to Prepare for an Interview

You have done your homework. You have sent out your résumé and your cover letter. You have even filled out the application. Now you receive a call: you are offered an interview in a week for the job of your dreams. What do you do now?

Rule 10. Be nosey. Find out how many applicants are being interviewed.

If I am offered an interview, I always ask how many candidates are being interviewed. I like to know my odds. If I am one of three or four, I know I have a better chance of getting the job than if ten applicants are being interviewed. Sometimes the employer is taken aback by the question, but usually the employer will tell me. If he or she won't tell me, I assume it is a high number. Once I was told the employer was interviewing two applicants. I figured I had a fifty-fifty chance, but I did not get the job. Apparently the employer did not like either of us and later opened up the applicant pool for more candidates. Knowing how many candidates an employer is interviewing can also help you decide if you want to continue pursuing the position, especially if you are expected to pay all or part of the interview expenses.

Rule 11. Find out what kind of interview it is.

There are preliminary or screening interviews, panel interviews, group interviews, stress interviews, and case scenario interviews. Some interviews are a combination of two or more of these types of interviews. It is nice to know what to expect and whether you are interviewing with one person or eight people.

Screening or Preliminary Interview

The preliminary or screening interview is usually by phone to see if you have the preliminary qualifications for the job, to see if you are still available, and to see if you are comfortable with the salary range. With this economy, an employer does not want to go through the whole process and then find out that its ideal candidate won't accept the salary offer. Sometimes the screening interview is done by the human resources department to determine if the candidate meets the criteria for the position. Then the supervisor or hiring officer does the second interview.

I had a preliminary screening panel interview. The whole interview process went like clockwork. There were ten applicants and five hours of interviews. My interview was at 9 a.m. The process consisted of two separate interviews; each one was thirty minutes long. At exactly 9:00 a.m., I was escorted into the room to be interviewed. There were eight panel members who each asked a question. At the end of the thirty minutes, I went into another room with eight more panelists who again each asked me a question. The whole process was done with military precision. I left the building, and that was the end of the interview. I had flown across the country for an hour interview with sixteen different people. I knew right away I did not get the job. Luckily, a good friend worked in the same city, and I was able to have lunch with her before I flew back home. I always wondered why this employer did not do such preliminary interviews on the phone.

Case Scenario Interview

This type of interview will give the applicant an exercise to complete, such as a case study or fact pattern with questions. In a regular type of interview, you usually answer a group of questions to say how you would do different parts of the job description. The purpose of the scenario interview is for the candidate to show how he or she would do part of the job. This type of interview can show how a candidate reacts under pressure and with time constraints.

When applying for a human resources job, I was given a case study and was told to determine whether the employer's conduct violated any discrimination laws and what advice I would give to the department head. It was very similar to a law school exam. This was part of the total interview process. I also had a group interview and a one-on-one interview with the hiring officer.

Panel Interview

A panel is an interview with several people who will interact with the position you are applying for in different ways. For example, there may be a representative from human resources, a department head, a member of the union, a member of the public, various committee members, and so forth. Each person will have a different interest in the position. Usually, each person gets to ask one question. A panel interview can be a screening interview (see above) after which the top applicants interview with someone else, such as the supervisor of the position, or it can also be used as the final interview. It is always helpful to know beforehand that you are interviewing with a group. Otherwise, it can be disconcerting if you are expecting a one-on-one interview and are ushered into a room with a large group of interviewers. When you are answering the questions in a panel interview, you need to look at the person asking the question and address your answer to him or her. However, you also need to look around occasionally and make eye contact with the other panelists. Sometimes a good answer for one person will be a bad answer for someone else, depending on his or her role at the company. For example a union committee member might like your answer, but the management representative might not.

Stress Interview
The stress interview is a type of interview designed to determine how the applicant reacts under stress. The interviewer may be antagonistic or bullying just to see how the applicant reacts under this type of pressure. The interviewer may arrive late or give the applicant the silent treatment just to see the reaction. This type of interview has often been used in sales, but it is not that common anymore. If you are subjected to this kind of interview, remember not to get frustrated and to keep your cool. Some applicants may choose not to work for a company that puts its applicants through such a process. You need to be on guard in all interactions with your future employer, even before the big interview. The employer may be testing your stress level at any time. If this happens to you, just smile. If you show frustration or annoyance to anyone, the interviewers will find out about it.

Group Interview
It used to be that one candidate rarely saw or interacted with another candidate. That used to be an unwritten rule of etiquette for interviews. Now you may even be at the same podium or at the same reception with all the other candidates. A group of candidates for the same position may be expected to mingle and introduce themselves to the stakeholders. This can be uncomfortable for the candidates, but it does save time and money for the employer. I guess the conventional wisdom is that if the person cannot handle this kind of situation, then he or she might not be the right person for

the job. This type of interview is often used for Department Heads and City Managers in the public sector.

Rule 12. Find out if the employer will pay your travel expenses.

What do you do if the company won't pay your travel expenses? Should you go for the interview anyway? This is a really tough question. On the one hand, you should be reluctant to pay out-of-pocket expenses. Normally I would be insulted if the company would not even pay my expenses for an interview, but with the bad economy, I have changed my mind if it is a job I really want. Some employers use this tactic to help the local candidates and to see how interested the out-of-town candidates really are. If you decide to pay your own way, keep good records since those expenses are tax deductible.

Do an analysis and ask the following questions:
1. Is it a great job?
If the answer is no, don't bother. If it is a fabulous job, you may want to consider it.
2. What are my chances or odds?
If you are one of two or three candidates, your chances are good; if are one of ten candidates, you might want to pass it up.
3. What is the actual cost to be interviewed?
If you live fairly close and the cost is two hundred dollars, maybe you will consider it. If the total cost is six hundred dollars, you may want to rethink the interview.
4. How long is the interview?
A long trip for an hour interview might not be worth it. An extensive all-day interview that involves meeting with several people may be worthwhile.
5. Will the company pay part of the expenses?
See if they will split the costs or offer to pay the air fare if the company will pay for the hotel. I had a job interview where the employer agreed to reimburse up to four hundred dollars. That was the cost of the flight. Because I was interested in the position, I decided to go ahead and pay the rest of the expenses. I did not get the job, but I was glad I went, because it turned out be a good learning experience and I got a tax deduction for going to Las Vegas.

Rule 13. *Make your own travel arrangements if you can.*

Because of a bad experience, I always like to confirm my own travel arrangements, especially if someone else has made them for me. See if the employer will pay for your expenses directly or whether you have to use your own credit card and be reimbursed later. Sometimes it can be a financial burden if you have to use your own credit card. I had applied for a job and the flight information was e-mailed to me with the reservation code. I presented this paper to the airline at check-in. They told me a reservation had been made, but that it was cancelled when payment had not been made in a timely manner. To make matters worse, the original flight was overbooked and the later flight cost seven hundred dollars. My first reaction was to forget the whole thing, thinking that if this company couldn't get my reservation right, maybe I didn't want to work for them. However, I was really interested in this position, so I decided to pay for the flight and hope for the best. The employer was very apologetic about the mistake and did reimburse me the total cost of the flight. I felt this incident showed my prospective employer that I was resilient when something unpleasant happened. I had a great interview; however, I did not get the job.

However, as a result of this experience, I always check with the airline in advance to make sure the reservation has not been cancelled. I don't want this to happen again. In fact, I prefer to make my own arrangements. The down side of this is that I may have to pay out-of-pocket expenses and it may take longer to be reimbursed. If I am given a dollar cap, then I will take the time to get the flight times and airline of my choice. I can also get frequent flyer miles.

Rule 14. *Be prepared.*

Google everyone and everything. First of all, this will let you find out who is interviewing you. It also gives me an idea of the roles of the interviewers. See what you can find on the internet about the people who will be interviewing you. See if you can find out their credentials and how long they have been at the company. A picture is nice too, so you can recognize them when you see them. When I was director of human resources for an electric company, we had a large group interview with several people called the training committee. One of the applicants later told me how shocked she was to enter a room full of ten people. She had assumed that she would be interviewing with the person she talked to on the phone.

You need to research the employer, the job itself, and the cutting-edge issues and concerns in this field. What did we do before the internet? Basically we had to go to the library, which often took too much time and effort for most of us. Now we just click, and the answers to our questions appear as if by magic. You know that the employer and HR staff are googling your name, so you should be googling them as well.

Google the name of the incumbent or predecessor of the job you are seeking. See if you can find out why that person left. Did she retire, or was she laid off? How long had she worked there? Check the archives of the local newspaper online. You might find a story in the newspaper about any problems or scandals. I had an interview with an employer where six or seven directors in the same department had left the company in the last five years. I knew this, but I chose to take the position anyway. I thought my situation would be different. Guess what? It wasn't.

Rule 15. Check the employer's website and its competitors' websites.

Check the employer's own website for information. I have often been surprised as to what I have been able to find. In one interview, I pulled out some organization charts when asked a question. The panel was very impressed and asked me where I got them. They were surprised when I told them I found them on its website. I have also found reports. Maybe you can find an annual report of the department where you are interviewing. If you don't find what you are looking for, ask the employer if it can share that information with you. This shows that you are seriously interested in the position.

You may also get some pertinent information by googling your employer's competitors' websites. You may be able to get some valuable information that you can use in your interview. Maybe they are doing something cutting edge that can be applied to your prospective company. If they ask you about ideas for being more competitive, they might be impressed if you know what their competition is doing. You may also get ideas about similar concerns in that industry.

Rule 16. Learn the buzz words.

It is important to know the vocabulary, jargon, or buzz words of the business for which you are applying. Attorneys speak a different language than accountants or engineers. For example, a lot of attorneys like to use Latin phrases like *caveat emptor* (let the buyer beware) and *quid pro quo* (this for that). If you are new to your field, you need to learn these terms and buzz words so that you understand them and can use them. For example, in human resources, all the names of the employment discrimination laws are known by letters: The ADA, ADEA, EEO, AA, Title VI, and Title VII. You need to be familiar with the terms and acronyms in your field. You don't want to ask what a term means in the interview. You may want to look at the website of a professional organization to learn some of these terms.

Chapter 3.

The Interview:
Details, Details, Details

Rule 17. Be on time.

The worst thing you can do in an interview is to be late. If you are late to the interview when you are trying to impress your prospective bosses, then you will probably be late to work at your prospective job. Being late is disrespectful. Even if you have an excuse for being late (flat tire, late train, lost cab), there really are no good excuses. Get an alarm clock and leave yourself plenty of time to anticipate the unexpected. You should really arrive at your destination about thirty minutes early. If you are a little early, then you can reward yourself by getting a coffee at a local café. If you get jittery with a cup or two of coffee, this might be the time to drink water instead.

Rule 18. Make sure you know the location of the interview.

This goes along with the rule above. You need to know where you are going, both literally and figuratively. Make sure you have the address and the telephone number of the person you are meeting, just in case you need last-minute instructions. Plug the address into your GPS in your car. Print out a Mapquest, too. Sometimes the GPS or the Mapquest is wrong, so it is good to have the address and telephone number. Do not rely on someone else to find the address for you, especially a taxi driver.

I stayed in a hotel in downtown Baltimore and hailed a cab to go to a union hall. I had printed a Mapquest that showed it would take less than ten minutes. After awhile, I got the feeling that we were taking a wrong turn. "Isn't that Washington?" I said. It turned out there were two streets with the same name, one a street and one an avenue. It also turned out the taxi driver was from another country, had recently moved to Baltimore, and had just started his taxi career. In addition, I had to explain what a union hall was. Finally I persuaded him to call taxi dispatch, who directed him to the right location. The good news is that I had left an hour early so that when I finally arrived with only two minutes to spare, no one knew that I had almost missed the meeting.

Rule 19. *Wear the right outfit for the interview.*

A nice suit with a tie that is not too distracting or too wide is always a good choice for a man. For women, it can get more problematic. Try to wear an outfit that you think would fit into the work environment of your prospective company. You might even want to check the company's website to see how other employees are dressed. Look at the picture of your prospective boss to see what he or she is wearing. A nice suit or a jacket is also a good choice for a woman. It should fit properly but not be too tight or revealing. If you think something may be too loud or bright, it probably is.

Of course, you need to know the culture of your prospective employer. At Google or Microsoft, employees dress much more casually. If you are interviewing at one of these companies, you do not want to overdress.

In the early days of my career as a woman lawyer, women were expected to dress like men, right down to the three-piece blue suit with a white shirt. Many women actually wore ties to go with this outfit. In those days women wore suits with skirts. Some judges did not even allow women attorneys to wear trousers to court. Now pantsuits are a staple of Secretary of State Hillary Clinton!

Rule 20. *Give the right handshake.*

In the era of hand sanitizers and H1N1 Influenza, some people don't like to shake hands, like Donald Trump. I still believe in a good handshake for both men and women. You have to have just enough oomph. A limp handshake is just wishy-washy and won't get anyone a job. A firm-but-not-too-firm handshake is just right. Don't be a bone crusher and be too rough with the other person. I have had people shake my hand who I really believed were trying to hurt me or prove that they were stronger than I was. If you are someone who does not like to shake hands, try it anyway. However, if you really can't muster a handshake, say something witty or relevant so you can go on with the interview with a modicum of dignity. "I would like to shake your hand, but I sprained my hand." "I would like to shake your hand, but my child is sick and I don't want to risk passing on the germs." You get the idea. While you are shaking hands, look the person in the eye and smile and say something pleasant. "It is nice to meet you." "What a nice office." "What a nice view!" "What a beautiful drive to get here." The most important things are the eye contact and the smile.

Rule 21. Be careful with the jokes.

An interview is serious business, but you should still try to have fun. It is an interview, not an execution, although sometimes it may feel like one. Try to get to know the interviewer(s) and bond with them. Cracking a joke can sometimes break the tension. Just make sure it is appropriate. Your future employer does not want to hear a joke that has a double entendre and is insulting to one of the people interviewing you. You have to find the right balance. Try to show your personality but don't be too outgoing. On the other hand, don't be boring and mumble in a monotone.

Rule 22. Don't assume the interviewer has read your résumé.

Don't assume that the interviewer has actually read your cover letter, résumé, or anything else you may have provided. Even though you have written a full explanation in your cover letter, don't be surprised if the questions cover what you have already included in your packet.

There are many explanations for this. Maybe the material did not get from human resources to the individual panel members. Even if it did, maybe the interviewers have not had the chance to read your information. Some interviewers may feel it is a waste of time preparing when they can just ask the applicant what they want to know.

If you get asked the obvious, don't roll your eyes. Consider this a second chance to convince the committee that you are the best candidate for the position. For example, I mentioned in a cover letter that I had written three award-wining books pertinent to the position. I was asked when the book was going to be published. I realized very quickly that the interviewer had not read my letter. However, it did give me an opportunity to toot my own horn and explain what the books were about and show how that skill set was related to the position.

Rule 23. Ask what you can do for the company.

Of course, I am paraphrasing the famous John F. Kennedy quote. It is your job to show the interviewer what you can do for the company, not what it can do for you. That is why talk of benefits and salary are usually not appropriate at the first round of interviews unless the employer brings them up. In this economy, you need to show the future employer why it needs you and how your experience and expertise are going to help it. This is where your research comes into play. You can show what you can bring to the table. You may be able to give some good suggestions on improvements that their competitors are using or suggest ways to save money.

Rule 24. Be observant.

The conventional wisdom is that a picture is worth a thousand words. While you are walking around the offices of your prospective employer, you are probably rehearsing your answers to hypothetical questions. You also need to be attentive and see what is going on behind the scenes. First impressions are not always correct, but they can give you a glimpse of what working at this company will be like. Look at the interaction between your prospective boss and associates. Observe whether the employees seem engaged. Usually a company will put its best foot forward for a prospective employee. If that is not happening, you may wonder why. What is the diversity of this employer? Who makes the coffee? Can you tell the management style of your future boss? This may be your future job, so you need to pay attention.

You need to be super vigilant about finding out everything you need to know about this company and more specifically about your boss and co-workers so that if you do get a job offer, you will be informed enough to make a good decision.

Rule 25. Never say you do not have any questions.

At some point in the interview, usually at the end, you will probably be asked if you have any questions. Never say you don't have any questions or that the company has already answered all of them. That shows a lack of interest. This is your chance to show you have some in-depth knowledge of the company and that you are genuinely interested in the position. This is generally not the time to ask about the compensation package.

I always make a list of questions the night before the interview and may add to it during the interview. Here are some questions to ask:

1. Ask questions about the organization chart. Who does the person in this position report to and who does your new boss report to?

2. What kind of training will be provided and who will do it?

3. Who was formerly in the position and why did they leave? This helps the candidate know if the incumbent retired or was fired or if this is a new position.

4. Ask what the company's expectations are for this position. This allows the applicant to see what the company is looking for and can respond accordingly.

5. Ask a question to clarify something that was on the employer's website, blog, or local newsletter. This shows you have done your homework.

6. What brought you to this company and what do you like best about working here? I love this question because you are doing the interviewing now but in a positive way.

7. What is your management style and how do you interact with your employees?

8. Where will my office be?

9. When will the position start?

10. What exactly will be my job duties? I have read the job description, I but don't know what the priorities are.

11. What will be my first big assignment?

12. What are the opportunities for advancement?

13. How has your business been affected by the economy? Have there been layoffs?

14. Who is your biggest competitor?

Chapter 4

How to Answer Interview Questions

Rule 26. Rehearse answers in advance.

Here are some questions with some possible answers to consider. You can adapt to your own circumstances to make them sound real. Try not to sound rehearsed in the interview.

1. Why are you interested in this position?

Always answer this question in terms of how your skills, knowledge and experience can help your potential employer. Show them your enthusiasm. Don't give answers that involve money or benefits at these preliminary questions. Save that for later.

Here are some different ways to answer this question:

1. I am uniquely qualified for this position and it is a culmination of my skills, education, and expertise. (There is symmetry in answering in threes.)

2. I have always wanted to work for a city, college, or hotel.

3. I have always wanted to live in central Florida. (However, the location should not be the first reason but maybe the third or fourth.)

4. I made a mistake by moving back to New England and want to move back to Florida as soon as possible.

5. Working for your company would be the pinnacle of my career.

6. With twenty years of prior experience, I believe I can bring some good ideas to this job.

7. These are challenging times, and I have some ideas about meeting these challenges that I would like to share.

8. This is not just a job for me. This is the place I want to be, and I am passionate about working in this field.

9. I know that your company has an excellent reputation and has some well-known experts in the field. I believe I have a lot to offer and will add to the progress that has already been made.

10. I have been planning for this job my whole life. I have the aptitude, the education, and the passion for this job. It is just a natural progression of all my previous experience.

2. Tell me about you and your background.

Give the condensed version. Give them your elevator speech first (the speech you give in an elevator to tell someone why they should hire you, which in most elevators will take about thirty seconds). The condensed version should have the same highlights that are in your cover letter. Do not start chronologically and go through each of your jobs and what you did. That is the purpose of a résumé. Be sure to highlight those areas in your background that are germane to the job description. Remember you want to get the employer's attention.

3. Why were you fired?

This is probably the hardest question to answer, but you have to do it. This is why some employees resign—so they never have to answer this question. There is a delicate balance between taking accountability and not blaming anyone else and making it bland enough that you can still be considered a viable candidate. If you were laid off, that is much easier to explain, since so many companies have eliminated positions or whole departments because of the economy. Here are some suggestions:

1. I was involved in a dispute with another employee. I lost my temper and was terminated. After that I went to an anger management class, which gave me some coping skills, and I know that will never happen again.

2. I had a problem with alcohol. I went to rehab and have been sober for two years. I have been working for two years, and I believe everyone deserves a second chance.

3. I was not fired; I was laid-off because of budgetary concerns. Our whole section was eliminated because of the economy.

4. There was some horseplay at work and it got out of hand. I was terminated. I went to counseling and learned how to deal with my emotions. I learned my lesson and believe I will be a better employee because of this.

5. I lied about something that I did. I regret doing that, and I have no one to blame but myself. That was ten years ago, and I feel I am a better person now because of this experience.

6. I spent some time in jail, and I believe I have paid my debt to society. I finished my degree while in jail and helped others to read. I have the experience and education for this position, and I won't let you down.

4. Why do you want to leave your current job?
This is a difficult question to answer but not as hard as why you were fired. This is really a tricky question, a sort of chicken and egg question. If the new job is a natural progression from the old job and is really a promotion with more money, that is fairly easy to explain. If you have been at the old job for less than a year, that can be a job-hopping problem. If you are having problems at the old job, you may need to be diplomatic about explaining these difficulties. Here are some suggestions:

1. I have stopped learning. I have been there five years and I am doing the same thing over and over. It is time to move on. I want a challenge, and I believe this job will provide that.

2. I love my job, but this new job is an opportunity with more responsibilities and more money. It is a natural progression of my experience and expertise.

3. I am ready for a challenge, and I believe this job provides that.

4. It is really not about leaving my old job; I see this as a great opportunity for my career. In addition, my widowed mother is sick and lives nearby.

5. What have you been doing since you were fired?
Somehow it is easier to get a job when you already have one, just as it is easier to get a loan when you already have money. The employer wants to see

that you have been using your time in a productive fashion. Here are some suggestions.

I. I went to Louisiana to help the cleanup effort and helped rescue birds that had been affected by the oil spill. I wanted to give back to the community.

2. I have been teaching some classes at the small business association to help other unemployed workers.

3. I have been rethinking the balance of work and family in my life and have decided to take a part-time position.

4. I have been a stay-at-home dad for the summer. I really enjoy it, but I am definitely ready to go back to work.

5. I have been taking some courses at the local college. That has really helped me keep my skills current.

6. Why do you want to work here?
The employer wants to know why you have selected this company. Whatever you answer, don't say anything about money or benefits. Here are some suggestions:

1. I have talked to friends that work here, and they always say that this is the best employer in the area.

2. Your engineering department is the best in the state, and I believe this is the best place to learn about my profession.

3. This is really my dream job. I have always wanted to work for your company after I got some experience elsewhere.

4. I like the job. I like the location. I like the people.

7. What do you like about your current job?
This is also a trick question. If you like your job so much, why are you looking? If you don't like your job, what is wrong with you? Here are some suggestions.

1. I learn something new every day, but I am ready for a change.

2. I like my boss and we have collaborated on a lot of projects. However, I have been working on the same projects for five years and am ready to move on.

3. I love working with my co-workers. There is a sense of family here. I want to leave the area to be closer to my parents, who need my help now that they are in their eighties.

8. What don't you like about your current job?

You can't really say anything bad about your job without it sounding like you are the one at fault and that you are a whiner. Here are some suggestions:

1. I have worked in the same department for ten years. I feel that I have learned as much as I can in this position. That is why I am looking elsewhere—to get some new experience and still use what I have learned here.

2. I like to work alone on my own projects. Here I am part of a large team. I would like the luxury of working on my own research. I believe this job offers those opportunities.

3. I feel that I am a creative person, and this job, by definition, does not allow me to use my creative side. I am very excited about the prospect of bringing new ideas to the table.

9. What would your boss say about you?

Never say anything bad about your current or past bosses, even if you feel they were the cause of any problems you had at work. Here are some answers.

1. My boss would say I am a good worker, that I am trustworthy, and that I will do whatever it takes to get the job done. He may also tell you that we have agreed to disagree about how the work should be done sometimes.

2. My boss and I did not always see eye-to-eye on certain projects. I think that is a positive thing, because he saw things that I missed and I saw things that he missed. He would say that I was loyal and dependable.

3. My boss and I have a good relationship. He knows I am interviewing today. He knows that I am looking for an opportunity to advance, and he agrees that there aren't any promotional opportunities where I am working.

10. What is your style of management?

Most companies do not want someone who will micromanage—that is, someone who cannot delegate and hovers around an employee telling him or her exactly how to do things. On the other hand, it doesn't want someone who can't deal with employee issues. Know your prospective company when you answer this question. This is a time when your research will be helpful. If you are applying at Google, the culture there is going to be much more laid back. In some stricter environments, micromanaging might be considered a strength. You can also name a type of management. Here are some suggestions:

1. I don't micromanage, but I meet regularly with my staff to stay informed about the status of their projects.

2. I try to delegate responsibility to my employees, but I let them know I am available if they need my help.

3. Some employees need more or less supervision. I try to adopt a plan suited to an employee's knowledge, experience, and personality.

4. Our employees are our greatest strength, and I like to delegate projects to them and let them work out the details.

5. At the end of the day, I am the one held accountable, so I get regular reports so I know if someone is off-track.

6. I expect employees to show initiative and be self-starters, but I have regular oversight.

7. I like to ask for my employees' opinions and get consensus, but at the end of the day, it is my decision.

8. I adhere to the One-Minute Manager strategy invented by Kenneth Blanchard and try to find employees doing something right.

9. I like Management by Walkabout. I like to get out into the field and see how the employees are doing on the job, and it helps me know what is going on.

11. What would your subordinates say about you?

How you treat your subordinates is as important as the relationship between you and your boss. Some employees have a great relationship with their bosses but don't treat their own employees fairly. Here are some suggestions.

1. My employees would say that I am fair. They would say I give an assignment and then let them take the initiative to complete it.

2. New employees would say that I explain the job and help them help with their first assignments. Once they are familiar with the department, I give them more and more responsibility.

3. They would say I am a good mentor and that I help them advance by giving them opportunities to take classes and go to conferences.

4. They would say that when there are problems, they feel comfortable coming to me to discuss them and come to an amicable solution.

12. What are your strengths?

This is not the time to be modest. This is the time to toot your own horn. This is a good way to highlight your achievements and experience. I always try to put in some integrity strengths such as fairness, honesty, and loyalty. As you go through your list, keep the job description in mind so you hit those strengths needed for the position as well. I always add a sense of humor, because it gives a sense of resiliency. Here are some good strengths:

1. I am well organized.

2. I have the knowledge and experience in the field necessary for the position.

3. I am dependable and will do all I can to get the job done.

4. I am a team player and get along with others.

5. I am able to delegate to others.

6. I am loyal and fair.

7. I like to mentor employees so that I can pass on what I have learned in the last twenty-five years. I learn a lot from them too.

8. I have a good sense of humor, which helps in stressful situations.

13. What are your weaknesses?

Don't ever say you cannot think of one. That just sounds arrogant. Be honest, but pick a relatively weak weakness. It is also good to say that you are working on your weakness or you have conquered it most of the time. Your interviewers don't want to know that sometimes you have tantrums, take a lot of time off, or that you don't get along with co-workers. If you are applying for a budget position, don't say you aren't good with numbers. This is an area where your preliminary research can help you. If you found out that your predecessor micromanaged, don't say your weakness is getting into everyone's projects. Here are some suggestions:

1. Sometimes I have too much on my plate and am stretched too thin. I am working on delegating some of these projects to others.

2. I am working on the balance between my work life and family life.

3. I used to do things myself rather than take the time to explain to others exactly what I wanted. Now I try to have more patience and take the time to explain and mentor so others can also learn.

4. Sometimes I am impatient, but I am learning the virtues of patience.

5. I can be a perfectionist, but I am taking measures to overcome this. I realize that everything I write does not have to be perfect to be acceptable.

14. What is your greatest success?

This is a good question to highlight your achievements. However, there are some pitfalls. Don't be smug or arrogant about the success of a project, especially if it was a team effort. You need to give credit to the team, too. You could say what you contributed to the total project and also give credit to others that helped in your success. Don't be overly modest, either. Here are some pointers:

1. Pick something that was clearly a success and highlight your skills.

2. Pick something recent. If you pick something twenty years ago, the employer is going to wonder what you have done lately.

3. Pick something important. You may have succeeded in many projects that are not that significant.

4. Pick something easy to explain. If complicated, give the short version.

5. Be sure to explain what you learned from this success.

15. What is your greatest failure?

As an interviewer, I have asked this question many times, and I have been surprised how many people just won't admit to a failure. Again you will sound arrogant if you say that you have never failed. The conventional wisdom is that you need to fail in order to achieve success. Try to think of a failure that taught you something so this type of mistake won't happen again. Interviewers ask this question to see how resilient you are and to see how you change course once you know something is not going to work.

You want to give a good example so you can emphasize how you resolved the issue or what you learned from it once it was exposed. Remember no one is infallible. The important thing is that you learned from it, that you accepted responsibility for it, and that you were able to resolve it at a later time. You can also show how you can change direction when a different approach needs to be taken. Here are some examples:

1. I did not fire someone when I should have. I let it go on too long. If that happened again, I would address the issue much sooner, because it won't go away on its own.

2. My plans for the project just failed. I did not pay enough attention to what was going on around me. I did not realize that our plan was just not working. Next time I will stay on top of what is going on and not rely on what people are telling me.

3. My project failed because the wrong employees were in charge. I did not realize they did not have the experience and knowledge to run it. Now I get more involved.

4. The project failed because we did not have enough funding. We made some errors in calculations. Fortunately, I was able to transfer some funds, but I almost lost my job. It made me realize how important budgeting is and that there are not unlimited funds, especially now.

5. We found a mistake in the drawings and instead of changing direction, we continued anyway. The project ultimately failed, and I learned a valuable

lesson. Sometimes it is better to stop and start all over again rather than continue on a path where it is almost impossible to succeed.

16. Tell me about your best boss.
When you are talking about your best boss, be sure not to offend your prospective boss. For example, if you get the feeling that your prospective boss likes to micromanage, you might not want to say how much you like working independently and without direction. This question may give you an opportunity to see whether you and your future boss are compatible.

1. I have had two or three best bosses. What sets them apart is that they had confidence in me.

2. She gave me assignments and let me complete them with my own initiative and timetable. Then she would review them and make suggestions.

3. I always felt we had a good working relationship because we understood each other. I knew what my job was and what his expectations were.

4. I knew that if I needed assistance, he would drop everything to help me.

17. Have you hired or fired someone and regretted it later?
Everyone has hired or fired someone and later wished he hadn't. When you give an example, be sure to spell out what you learned from this bad decision and what you would do differently if this happens again.

1. Yes, I have hired someone and regretted it later. I promoted someone within the department. Although he did not have the requisite education and experience, I made an exception because I thought his years of experience at the company would be enough to learn the job. That was not the case. The employee was never able to get the skills and knowledge necessary to perform the minimum qualifications of the job. I regretted not trying to hire an employee outside the company who already had the proper experience.

2. There was a situation where one person was fired and the other was not. I regretted not firing both of them because it appeared that the company was selectively enforcing the discipline policy. There was horseplay, and I thought one person was responsible for starting it. Later on, I realized that it was unacceptable conduct for both employees and I should have fired both of them.

18. Where do you want to be in five years?

The answer to this can be delicate. You want to show healthy ambition, but you don't necessarily want the boss to think you are gunning for her job, at least not right away. You also don't want to say that you are only staying until you find a better job. The point of this question is to see whether you are a job hopper or whether you will stay a reasonable period of time. If you are asked how long you think you will stay at the company, five years is a good minimum. Try not to give a specific number of years. The important point is that you don't want to be stagnant and not growing in the same position for five years. Here are some suggestions:

1. I hope to stay here for my whole career until I retire.

2. I plan to be here for at least ten years.

3. I plan to master this job for a few years and then advance through the company.

19. How do you answer those whacky questions?

Some employers like to ask whacky questions. Remember when Barbara Walters asked Katherine Hepburn what kind of tree she would like to be? When you get a whacky question, you just have to wing it. See if you can give a humorous answer without appearing flakey or insincere; I found that's a good way to clear the air. If you don't understand the question, you can say you don't quite understand the question. Maybe they could rephrase?

20. Have you ever been terminated?

If you were ever terminated, you must be truthful about it if you want the job. You have to assume that the company will discover this information anyway, and it is better if it hears the details from you. This way you can explain what happened in the best light and what you learned from it.

Make sure that your answer is consistent with the background record the company may have and with the employment application you filled out for this job. On the employment application, the employer usually asks you why you left each position. At the end of the application, there is usually a statement that everything you say is true and correct and that not answering truthfully is grounds for termination. Even if you get the job, you can be immediately terminated later on if the employer finds out you lied on the application.

If you resigned, you may want to clarify why you left. Maybe your family moved, your parents were ill, or you were denied a promotion. Don't put yourself in a position where the company will get information that will contradict your version of what happened. If it was a forced resignation, you might as well explain it upfront. Otherwise it can just be embarrassing, and you probably won't get the job anyway.

21. Have you ever been convicted of a crime?
Many applications will ask whether you have been convicted of a felony in the last seven or ten years. If you have been convicted of a felony outside the seven or ten-year period, you can respond no. If you have been convicted of a misdemeanor only, you can respond no. If you have only been arrested but not convicted, that is also a no. Being arrested cannot be held against you. However, if you have recently been arrested and it has not been resolved yet and you are awaiting trial, you should tell your prospective employer.

Some applications ask if you have been convicted of a crime, which includes misdemeanors and felonies. If the employer sees something in a criminal history check, it is going to look at the specifics of the felony or crime and how long ago it occurred. If it was a youthful indiscretion like joyriding, the company is more likely to minimize it. However, if it was a recent conviction, that can have a negative impact on your chances of employment. Again you need to explain what happened and try to put it in the best light without lying.

22. Have you ever done anything that would embarrass your employer?
If you have been involved in something unethical or used bad judgment, you need to be honest about it. You have to expect a criminal history check, a check of local newspaper stories, and reference checks (and not just the names you gave them). They will google your name and check your social media accounts on sites like Facebook and MySpace. If you dressed up for Halloween in a skimpy costume and put it on Facebook, your judgment may be questioned, especially if alcohol or drugs were involved.

23. If you get the job, what would you do on the first week of the job?
Most employers want someone to hit the ground running with a plan. You need to give some specifics. However, you don't want to seem like a know-it-all who assumes that there are a lot of problems and you are the only one with good ideas to fix them. You don't want your answers to sound arrogant.

1. I would get to know the staff and find out what their concerns are.

2. I would read everything I could find, including the personnel manual, to learn the policies, procedures, and culture of the company.

3. I would meet with my boss and see what projects she has for me and prioritize them.

4. I would not make any changes in the first weeks. I would just listen and observe so I know what is going on.

24. Do you have the experience that this job needs?
If this is your first job after college, you need to show how your extracurricular activities, volunteer work, college courses, and summer internships give you the skills and experience needed for the job for which you are applying. Everyone has had a first position, and you have to show why you will make a good employee. Remember you are telling your future employer what you can bring to the table. Even if you have been a stay-at-home mom or dad with little or no work experience, try to relate your organization and time-management skills to the position for which you are applying. These are called transferable skills. Many employers have the philosophy that they are looking for a certain kind of person, such as someone with energy, enthusiasm, and initiative. They are willing to train that kind of person to give him or her the skills needed for the job.

25. What are your hobbies?
You want to show you have hobbies and interests, but on the other hand, you don't want to appear too bold. List some sports to show you exercise and give a couple of interests, such as movies, golf, and travel.

26. Expect the question you don't want to answer. You know what it is.
After Tim Russert died, many of his guests on *Meet the Press* said that he usually asked the one question that the guest did not want to answer. He did his research and knew what that one question was. It was usually a scandal or newspaper article that was contradictory to something the person had said previously. That is why his guests had to be prepared to answer that question.

For example, if you were fired from your last job, you need to get your version out there to explain what happened. It is so much better to be upfront about it. If you were fired, explain the circumstances in the best light. For example, many city managers get terminated after an election when they lose some of their political support. If that is what happened to you, explain the political context and the timing after the election. If you had a DUI ticket and there was a story in the newspaper about it, explain what happened and say what you learned from it.

Chapter 5

INTERVIEWING AND THE LAW

Rule 27. Know whether you are in a protected category.

It is important that you know the laws prohibiting discrimination so you will know whether the interview questions are legal or illegal. Here is a list of the protected categories. (For further information about each of the protected categories and the federal laws prohibiting discrimination, see Appendix C.)

1. **Race**
2. **Color**
3. **National Origin**
4. **Sex, Pregnancy, and Marital Status**
5. **Religion**
6. **Age**
7. **Disability**
8. **Veteran**
9. **Sexual Orientation and Gender Identity Discrimination**
10. **Genetic Discrimination**

As an applicant, you are covered by federal, state, and local discrimination laws. Before we cover the protected categories, I would like to look at the theories of discrimination. Discrimination is nothing more than making distinctions or differentiations. If someone is told she has discriminating tastes, that is considered a compliment, but if someone is accused of being discriminatory in the human resources department, it is probably meant as an insult. It is important to remember that employment discrimination does not cover all unfair practices. It only covers those practices that are prohibited by discrimination laws.

To allege discrimination, an applicant must show two things: 1) that the applicant was in a protected classification, and 2) that the employer's conduct was discriminatory. There are basically two type of discrimination: disparate treatment and adverse impact.

1. Disparate Treatment
Disparate treatment means that a person in a protected category is treated differently from another person not in a protected category. Disparate treatment is intentional discrimination. In order to show disparate treatment, comparison is the key. This is done by comparing the employee with another employee in another similarly situated position to see if the treatment is, in fact, different. Here are some examples of disparate treatment:

A. A woman bank teller with identical qualifications is hired at a lower salary than a man.

B. An African American manager must wait one year before taking a vacation, but a white manager must wait only six months before taking a vacation.

C. Two employees are caught stealing from the employer's cash register. The Hispanic employee is fired and the white employee is suspended for two days.

All three of these examples are disparate treatment discrimination. If both bank tellers were hired at the same salary, both management trainees had to wait a year to take vacation, and both employees were fired, it would not be discriminatory.

2. Adverse Impact
The second theory of discrimination, adverse impact, is more subtle than disparate treatment. While disparate treatment is discriminatory or intentional on its face, adverse impact is neutral on its face but discriminatory in its impact or effect. Here are some examples:

A. No one with an arrest record will be hired.
The rule seems neutral, but statistics show that African Americans statistically have a higher arrest record than whites. Even though the rule is neutral, the rule is objectionable because it has a discriminatory impact on a protected class and is also not job related. The employer needs to show there is a legitimate business reason for the rule. Is there a business necessity to make those who have been arrested ineligible for employment? Since arresting someone is so

preliminary, and the charges might never be filed, the person may never be convicted anyway. A better rule would be to look at conviction records, not arrest records. Therefore, this policy has no legitimate business reason and must be discriminatory.

B. If both spouses work for the same employer, only one can work full time. A company's anti-nepotism policy does not allow both spouses to work full time. This is neutral on its face but may have a disparate impact on women. Let's assume there are ten pairs of spouses that work for this employer and that nine of the spouses that work full time are the husbands. This is a neutral rule on its face, but it has a discriminatory impact on the wives. There is no legitimate job-related reason for this policy, and therefore it is an example of disparate impact discrimination.

3. Pretext for Discrimination
If the employer is able to show there is a legitimate business reason for the policy, then the employee or prospective employee has the opportunity to show that the reasons given were not job related but a pretext for discrimination.

The company that had the policy of not hiring applicants with an arrest record did not have a good reason or business necessity for the policy. For that reason, it could be presumed that that policy was just a pretext or an excuse to discriminate against minorities. In the second example, there really was no good reason for making one spouse work full time and one part time, and it could be said that policy was a pretext for discriminating against women. It seems as though there were other solutions that would not have the same impact. They could have required spouses to work in different departments or prohibited one spouse from supervising another. Those would have been good job-related reasons for the policy.

4. Accommodation
In the area of religion, disability, and, under certain circumstances, pregnancy, it is not enough to just prohibit discrimination. An employer can be required to accommodate an employee's religion, disability, and (in some cases) pregnancy. See the section under pregnancy, religion, and disability below for a more in-depth discussion of accommodation.

Title VII of the Civil Rights Act of 1964
This landmark legislation, Title VII, prohibits discrimination in five categories: race, color, national origin, religion, and sex.

Race and Title VII
According to the Equal Employment Opportunity Commission, (EEOC), the agency that enforces Title VII, there are five racial categories under Title VII:
1. **White (not of Hispanic origin):** All persons having origins in any of the original peoples of Europe, North Africa, or the Middle East.
2. **Black (not of Hispanic origin):** All persons having origins in any of the black racial groups of Africa.
3. **Hispanic:** All persons of Mexican, Puerto Rican, Cuban, Central or South American, or other Spanish culture or origin, regardless of race.
4. **Asian or Pacific Islander:** All persons having origins in any of the original peoples of the Far East, Southeast Asia, the Indian Subcontinent, or the Pacific Islands. This area includes, for example, China, India, Japan, Korea, the Philippine Islands, and Samoa.
5. **American Indian or Alaskan Native:** All persons having origins in any of the original peoples of North America and who maintain cultural identification through tribal affiliation or community recognition.

All employees and applicants are in the protected category of race, including whites or Caucasians.

Color and Title VII of the Civil Rights Act of 1964
Discrimination on the basis of color under Title VII is usually synonymous with race discrimination. For example, a person who is discriminated against on the basis of color is usually also being discriminated against on the basis of race (African-American) or national origin (dark Hispanics or Indians), but discrimination on the basis of color is not always discrimination on the basis of race or national origin. An employer who hired a light-complexioned African American over a better-qualified dark-complexioned African American would be discriminating on the basis of color but not race. Title VII does not specifically define color, but the courts and the EEOC use the commonly understood meaning of color to include pigmentation, complexion, or skin shade or tone. Color discrimination occurs when a person is discriminated against based on the lightness, darkness, or other color characteristic of the person. Title VII prohibits race and color discrimination against all persons, including Caucasians.

National Origin and Title VII of the Civil Rights Act of 1964
The term national origin is more broadly defined than sex, race, or age. It includes the place where one is born or where an ancestor was born as well as the language or cultural qualities of an ethnic group. An applicant cannot

be rejected because of his or her surname, and a woman cannot be rejected because she is married to a Hispanic person or has a Spanish surname. National origin discrimination often involves Hispanics, although many other groups are, of course, covered too. The only way to require national origin for a position is if it is a bona fide occupational qualification (BFOQ), such as an actress or actor who is supposed to play a character of a specific nationality. The BFOQ provision is very narrowly construed by the courts.

All employees and applicants are protected from discrimination based on their national origin and ancestry.

Immigration Reform and Control Act of 1986
National Origin and the Immigration and Reform Control Act of 1986

The Immigration and Reform Control Act (IRCA) was adopted to control unauthorized immigration to the United States. However, the Office of Civil Rights prosecutes employers who discriminate on the basis of national origin or citizenship status. Employers with fifteen employees will already be covered by Title VII of the Civil Rights Act of 1964, which also prohibits national origin discrimination. But smaller employers with four or more employees, but less than fifteen employees, are prohibited from discriminating on the basis of citizenship status, which occurs when adverse employment decisions are made based upon an individual's real or perceived citizenship or immigration status. An employer refusing to hire refugees or people granted asylum is an example of citizenship discrimination.

Job Interview Questions

The most important thing you should know about job interview questions is that they should be job related. If all your questions are job related and have a business necessity, they will be proper questions. If they are not job related, most likely they will be improper questions. Here are some improper interview questions.

1. Improper Questions about Race
A. Are you Asian?

An interviewer cannot ask a question about an applicant's race, as this is prohibited by Title VII. Asians and Pacific Islanders are one of the five groups recognized by the EEOC.

B. Are you really an American Indian? What tribe?

Again, a prospective employer cannot ask a question about an applicant's race or national origin, which is prohibited by Title VII. American Indians and Alaska Natives are one of the five groups recognized by the EEOC.

C. What race is your spouse?

Asking about a spouse or relative's race is also prohibited by Title VII.

D. What is your race? I can't tell by looking at you.

This is a violation of Title VII. The only time a question like this can be asked is after you are already hired. An employer can ask you to voluntarily declare what race you are. This is needed for Equal Employment Opportunity (EEO) reports filed by employers.

E. Are you biracial?

No questions about race are allowed except, as mentioned above, as part of a voluntary request for EEO Report purposes. Identification Form EE0-1 asks participants to check which ethnic group with which they identify. In addition, it also allows participants to check if they identify with two or more of the five races (not Hispanic or Latino.)

2. Improper Questions about Color
A. Are you African American or do you have a sun tan?

This question is about race and color discrimination and is prohibited by Title VII.

B. Are you African American? You seem very light for an African American.

This question is both race and color discrimination and is prohibited by Title VII.

3. Improper Questions about National Origin
A. What kind of accent is that?

Trying to determine where someone is from by accent is prohibited by Title VII.

B. Where were you born? Where were your parents born?

Asking where an applicant or his or her parents were born is never job related and is national origin discrimination prohibited by Title VII. An interviewer may think he or she is just making conversation, but this is not an appropriate question. A prospective employer can only ask whether you can work in the United States, either yes or no.

C. What is your native language?
An interviewer cannot ask a question about an applicant's native language. This is national origin discrimination prohibited by Title VII. The interviewer can ask an applicant to list the languages he or she speaks and can ask what proficiency he or she has in those languages but, the interviewer cannot ask how the applicant happens to know those languages.

D. Where did you learn your English?
Again, an employer cannot ask indirectly what cannot be asked directly. This is not job related. An interviewer can ask if an applicant can speak English and at what level or proficiency but not where you learned it.

E. That is an interesting surname. Is that Hispanic?
This is national origin discrimination. An interviewer cannot ask questions about a surname even if he or she thinks it is small talk.

F. Where were your grandparents born?
Questions about ancestry and national origin are prohibited by Title VII. Again, an employer cannot ask you indirectly what it cannot cast directly.

Sex and Title VII
An employer cannot make hiring decisions based on the sex of its employees and applicants. When Title VII was first passed, sex was added as one of the categories at the last minute by Representative Howard W. Smith of Virginia. Some say it was a joke, but others disagree. The early airline cases show the history of sex discrimination. Flight attendants were forced to resign or retire if they got married, wore eye glasses, gained weight, got pregnant, or turned thirty-two. In addition, they were subjected to sexist taglines like "Fly Me." Slowly these policies were overturned once Title VII was in place.

The only way to legally restrict a job to one sex is if it is a bona fide occupational qualification (BFOQ). The employer must show that hiring only men or women for a particular job is reasonable and necessary to the operation of the business. This BFOQ exception has been very narrowly construed and has only included categories such as actress, model, restroom attendant, or sperm donor.

Sex and the Equal Pay Act of 1963
The Equal Pay Act requires that men and women in the same workplace be given equal pay for equal work. The jobs don't have to be identical but must be substantially equal. The job descriptions must be examined. In addition to salaries, overtime, bonuses, life insurance, vacation, training, reimbursement for travel,

and benefits must also all be the same. If there is an inequity, the wages of the higher-paid employee cannot be reduced, but the lower-paid employee has to get an increase. An aggrieved employee can sue directly in court and does not have to go through the EEOC. However, a claim under the Equal Pay Act will also be a claim of sex discrimination under Title VII. The time limits for filing for both laws are within two years of the alleged unlawful compensation. However, if there is a willful violation, the employee will have three years to file. The proposed Paycheck Fairness Act, which would amend the Equal Pay Act, was rejected by the Senate by a vote of 52-47 on June 5, 2012. It may be voted on again later in the session, depending on the election results in November 2012.

When you get a salary offer, try to find out if someone of the other sex in an equivalent position is making more than you. If you are a woman, you may have an Equal Pay Act claim and a Title VII claim. However, be careful that you are comparing every part of the job: your qualifications, your salary, you experience, and your time on the job.

While Title VII prohibits sex discrimination against men and women, the Equal Pay Act only protects women. If you are a man under these circumstances, you would only be covered by Title VII.

Sex and the Lily Ledbetter Fair Pay Act
The Lily Ledbetter Fair Pay Act amends Title VII of the Civil Rights Act of 1964 so that the 180-day statute of limitations for filing an equal-pay lawsuit regarding pay discrimination resets with each discriminatory paycheck. The Lily Ledbetter Fair Pay Act was signed into law on January 29, 2009. It was the first legislation that President Obama signed. The effective date of the law is May 28, 2007, one day before the date the Supreme Court issued its ruling. The purpose of the legislation was to reinstate the law that was overruled in *Ledbetter v. Goodyear Tire and Rubber Co.* This law allows an employee who did not know of the discrimination for many years to still be able to file a complaint after she finds out.

In 1979, Lily Ledbetter, the plaintiff, started working at Goodyear Tire and Rubber Company in Gadsden, Alabama. During her years at the factory, she was a salaried worker. She started at the same salary as the men, but by retirement, she was only earning $3,727 per month compared to the fifteen men who earned from $4,286 to $5,236 per month. She did not know about the discrimination until after she took early retirement and filed suit at that point. The Supreme Court held that she should have filed when the discrimination first occurred even though she did not know about it. Congress reinstated the law so that whenever an employee receives a discriminatory paycheck, the 180-day deadline to file is extended.

Sex and Title IX of the Educational Amendments of 1972

Title IX of the Educational Amendments prohibits sex discrimination in education. It covers any educational program or activity receiving federal funds. This landmark legislation incorporated the principles of Title VI and Title VII into education. Athletics proved to be the most controversial aspect of Title IX. It allowed women athletes to have parity with men athletes in both high schools and colleges. When Title IX came into effect, I was working at a traditional state women's college that had recently gone coed. We had to review every aspect of campus life to see if men had parity with women. At the time, no one really knew the impact the legislation would have. The law is enforced by the Office of Civil Rights of the US Department of Education. The remedy was only the ability to cut off federal funds, but that was enough to get the schools to comply.

Sex and the Pregnancy Discrimination Act

The Pregnancy Discrimination Act, which amends Title VII, was passed to prohibit pregnancy discrimination. An employer cannot refuse to hire a pregnant woman because she is pregnant or has medical issues because of the pregnancy or because of any bias of co-workers, clients, or customers. A pregnancy is to be treated the same as any other temporary disability another employee might have.

Pregnant women can work as long as they want during the pregnancy as long as they can perform the duties of the job. The employer cannot make women take a leave until the baby is born. The employer must keep open the pregnant woman's job or similar job as long as it would keep open the job of anyone else who is sick or on disability. Employers who provide health insurance must provide pregnancy insurance, and unmarried women and married women are treated the same in this regard.

You will have to make your own decision as to when to tell your employer that you are pregnant. I took a job when I was pregnant and did not tell anyone until someone asked me in the seventh month. This was before the Pregnancy Discrimination Act was passed. Since I had no protection, I decided not to tell anyone. Today, however, it does make sense to tell your employer so you can plan your time off.

Pregnancy and the Family Medical Leave Act
Pregnancy is covered by the Family Medical Leave Act (FMLA), and an employer must provide up to twelve weeks of unpaid leave to employees who either have a serious health condition or care for a seriously ill family member. The birth of a child and complications relating to childbirth or pregnancy would qualify as a serious health condition under FMLA. Adoption, postpartum conditions, and parental leave for childcare may also qualify.
There are three different types of leave under FMLA for pregnancy.
1. Pregnancy leave for pregnancy can be taken by women only.
2. Parental leave can be taken by men and women.
3. Parental leave can be taken intermittently if the employer allows it.

Marital Status and Sate Law
Although marital status discrimination is prohibited under federal law, it is a protected category in almost half of the states, including Florida where I live. Check with your state Human Rights Commission and see what is covered in your state. Check Appendix D for a list of state Fair Employment Commissions.

Sexual Orientation and Gender Identity
Although it could be argued that sexual orientation discrimination is a kind of sex discrimination, federal law does not prohibit sexual orientation discrimination. However, about twenty-two states prohibit sexual orientation discrimination. Gender identity discrimination is only prohibited in fifteen states at this time. If your state law does not prohibit sexual orientation discrimination, check if there are local county or city laws that prohibit sexual orientation discrimination.

Florida does not have a state statute on sexual orientation, but Broward County, Monroe County, Key West, Miami Beach, Oakland Park, West Palm Beach, and Gainesville have local ordinances for both gender identity and sexual orientation discrimination. Miami Dade, Fort Lauderdale, Palm Beach Gardens, Orlando, Tampa, Sarasota, St. Petersburg, and Pinellas County only prohibit sexual orientation discrimination.

At this time gay marriage is legal in Massachusetts, Connecticut, Iowa, Vermont, Washington, New York, Maryland, and Washington, D.C. In addition, Rhode Island will recognize gay marriages that were performed legally elsewhere. If passed, the proposed Employment Nondiscrimination Act (ENDA) would prohibit discrimination on the basis of sexual orientation and gender identity.

4. Improper Questions about Sex
A. What does your spouse think of your working nights or traveling?
There is no job-related reason to ask this. This goes back to more patronizing times when an employer wanted to know what the husband thought about his wife working at nights or traveling. Asking what your spouse thinks is not job related; an employer cannot even ask if you have a spouse.

B. What is your spouse's salary?
This is not job related. In the past, a woman might have been offered a lower salary if her husband was making a good salary.

C. Do you have any children?
Asking any questions about children is not job related. There are many stereotypes that women might have more absences if they are caring for a sick child. An employer can only ask if you can work the hours in the job description.

D. Are you pregnant?
Asking a woman if she is pregnant is not job related and is prohibited by sex discrimination laws.

E. Are you planning on having children?
This question is not job related and is prohibited by Title VII. It could be sex discrimination, because there are certain stereotypes about women and children in the workplace that cause women not to be taken seriously because they have these other responsibilities.

F. What is your marital status?
There is really no job-related reason to know whether someone is single, divorced, married, or widowed, especially at a job interview. What is job-related about someone's marital status? If you ask questions about marital status to both sexes, it is not prohibited by Title VII. However, it is a protected category in many states, including Florida, where I live. However, this is still very common on applications. If the purpose of asking marital status is to figure out how to address you, then as an alternative, an employer can just ask for preferred form of address: Ms., Mr., Mrs., Dr., other. That is short, simple, and not illegal.

G. Are you planning on adopting?
This is also prohibited discrimination.

H. When you have children, are you going to quit so you can stay at home with them?
There is no obligation to answer these kinds of questions. They are based on stereotypes of women in the workplace and are clearly a violation of Title VII.

Religion and Title VII of the Civil Rights Act
An employer cannot make a hiring decision based on an applicant's religion unless religion is a bona fide occupational qualification for the job. For example, a religious organization may refuse to hire or promote someone not embracing the same religious beliefs. Title VII protects all aspects of religious belief, observation, and practice. It is not limited to traditional religions like Christianity, Judaism, Islam, or Buddhism.

An employer is required to make reasonable accommodation for the religious beliefs of an employee or prospective employee unless it would create an undue hardship. Under Title VII, that hardship cannot pose more than a "*de minimis* cost or burden." This is a much lower standard for an employer to meet than the undue hardship under the Americans with Disabilities Act. The employer can consider the type of workplace, the nature of the employee's duties, the cost of the accommodation, and the number of employees needing the accommodation. Some examples are shift swaps for religious observance, making an exception to dress codes, and use of the work facility for religious observance.

An employer must make reasonable accommodation for an employee's religious beliefs unless it would be an undue hardship. If the cost is more than *de minimis*, then it is an undue hardship. The most common cases in this area are employees who cannot work on their Sabbath, particularly if that Sabbath is Saturday. Although most of the cases involve work schedules, an employer must also accommodate an employee's religious beliefs in the following areas as long as it is not an undue hardship. If the cost is small, then the employer must pay it. If the expense is large, especially for a small company, then there does not have to be accommodation. Here are some examples of accommodation:
A. Prayer breaks
B. Religious dietary requirements
C. Nonworking mourning periods
D. Modes of dress
E. Grooming habits

F. Religious scruples against joining a union

All religions with good faith beliefs are included under Title VII. Even atheists and agnostics can be covered by Title VII.

5. Improper Questions about Religion

A. What is your religion? Does your religion prevent you from working certain days?

There is really no job-related reason to know someone's religion. If an employer wants to know when you can work, it should have nothing to do with stereotypes of religion. It should just ask, "Can you work Saturdays and Sundays?"

B. Do you believe in God?

An employer cannot ask about your beliefs. They only have to be sincerely held.

C. What would Jesus do?

Any questions about religion are illegal.

D. Are you a Buddhist?

An interviewer cannot ask what religion someone is. This is protected by Title VII of the Civil Rights Act.

E. Will you be wearing a head scarf?

Generally a question like this is prohibited by Title VII. However, if a scarf was a true hazard (it might get caught in a machine), it might be an appropriate question only for that limited purpose.

E. How many times do you pray each day?

This is not job related. If someone asks for accommodation, an employer might be able to ask such a question in order to determine how the employee could pray at work.

Age and the Age Discrimination in Employment Act of 1967

An employer cannot discriminate on the basis of age against someone forty or older. There are more and more employees and applicants delaying retirement since their nest eggs have gotten smaller because of the downturn of the economy. If you are an older applicant, there are some buzz words to look for. If an employer says you are overqualified, that is an indication it may be discriminating against you on the basis of age. My view is that there is no such thing as being overqualified. If you have lots of experience for a position, assure the employer that you are interested in the position and want to stay with it for a few years. Tell them that you can hit the ground running because you have done work similar to this before. If you are willing to take a lower salary because you are also getting Social Security, say so. Older employees are particularly vulnerable during layoffs. An employer has to make sure that such action does not have an adverse impact on older employees.

Age and State Laws
Although age discrimination is covered under Title VII, it only covers employees forty and over. Most state laws cover age discrimination in employment and mimic the federal law. However, some states like Iowa, Kansas, New Jersey, New York, Oregon, and Vermont cover employees at age eighteen.

Proposed Legislation: Protecting The Older Workers Against Discrimination Act
This legislation overrules *Gross v. FBL Financial Services.* In the Gross case, the Plaintiff was fifty-three years old, and he was demoted and his duties were transferred to an employee in her forties. Gross then filed a claim under the Age Discrimination in Employment Act. At trial, the jury was instructed that if age was a motivating factor in the demotion, the verdict should be for the plaintiff. The plaintiff won, but FBL appealed based on the jury instruction. The Supreme Court held in a 5-4 decision that a mixed-motive jury instruction is not available to the plaintiff in an ADEA case. The proposed legislation would have the same mixed-motive protection that is included under Title VII. The latest version was introduced in the Senate on March 13, 2012.

Improper Questions about Age
A. How old are you?
Asking applicants how old they are or when they were born is not job related and is prohibited by the Age Discrimination in Employment Act. There is no mandatory retirement anymore, and it is not relevant to any hiring decision. However, an employer can ask age after the applicant has accepted the position for health insurance and pension purposes.

B. When were you born?
An employer can't ask something indirectly that cannot be asked directly under the ADEA.

C. What year did you graduate from high school?

Again, knowing the graduation year would allow an employer to figure out an applicant's age and is therefore improper and prohibited by the ADEA.

D. Don't you think you are too old for this position?

This is blatant age discrimination. You cannot be too old for a position, and this is a violation of the ADEA.

E. Don't you think you should make way for new blood?

New blood is code for age discrimination and is prohibited by the ADEA.

F. When are you planning on retiring?

An employer cannot ask when someone is going to retire or suggest that they retire, and this is prohibited by the ADEA.

G. Are you a grandparent?

There is no job-related reason to be asking this, and it can be a violation of the ADEA.

Americans with Disabilities Act

If you have a disability, you are not obligated to tell your employer about it. However, if you need reasonable accommodation to perform the job duties, then of course you will need to tell your employer and ask for accommodation. When you are applying for positions, the employer should never mention your disability, even if it is obvious because, for example, you are in a wheelchair.

The Americans with Disabilities Act (ADA) retains the basic definition of *disability* as an impairment that substantially limits one or more major life activities, a record of such an impairment, or being regarded as having such an impairment. However, it changes the way that these statutory terms should be interpreted in several ways. The effect of these changes makes it easier for an individual seeking protection under the ADA to establish that he or she has a disability within the meaning of the ADA. The act emphasizes that the definition should be construed in favor of broad coverage of individuals to the maximum extent permitted by the terms of the ADA and generally shall not require extensive analysis.

The standard for accommodation under the ADA is undue hardship. The Department of Labor will focus on the resources and circumstances of the employer in relation to the cost or difficulty of providing a specific accommodation. If it is too expensive or disrupts the nature or operation of the business, then it is undue hardship. This assessment is done on a case by case basis by the employer. Large corporations are going to be held to a higher standard than very small businesses. This is a higher standard than for religious accommodation under Title VII, which is *de minimis.*

Disability and the Family Medical Leave Act
The Family Medical Leave Act (FMLA) helps employees balance their work and family responsibilities by allowing them to take reasonable unpaid leave for certain family and medical reasons. The FMLA applies to all public agencies, all public and private elementary and secondary schools, and companies with fifty or more employees. These employers must provide an eligible employee with up to twelve weeks of unpaid leave each year for any of the following reasons:
1. For the birth and care of the newborn child of an employee
2. For placement with the employee of a child for adoption or foster care
3. To care for an immediate family member (spouse, child, or parent) with a serious health condition
4. To take medical leave when the employee is unable to work because of a serious health condition

Pregnancy and the ADA
Pregnancy by itself is generally not considered a disability under the Americans with Disabilities Act (ADA), because it generally does not meet the definition of disability since it is a temporary condition. However, some pregnant women may have complications that develop as a result of the pregnancy and develop diabetes, back problems, or high blood pressure. Therefore, women who work during pregnancy may be required to have job accommodations during and after their pregnancies.

Improper Questions about Disability

A. What is wrong with you?
Asking any question about health or disability is prohibited by the Americans with Disabilities Act. An employer can only ask an applicant if he or she can perform the job duties with or without reasonable accommodation.

B. Why are you in that wheelchair?
This is strictly prohibited by the Americans with Disabilities Act.

C. Have you ever filed a workers compensation claim?
This is not job related and cannot be asked before hiring an applicant.

D. What disease do you have?
It is unlawful to ask any questions about an applicant's disabilities.

E. What is your prognosis?
None of this information is job related for an applicant.

F. What kind of accommodation do you need?
It is up to the applicant or employee to ask for accommodation, but the request can be informal.

G. Can you perform the essential duties of this job without accommodation?
This is inappropriate. However, an employer can ask this question: "Can you perform the essential duties of this job with or without reasonable accommodation?"

F. Who is your doctor?
This is not job related for an applicant.

G. How is your mental health?
Mental health as well as physical health is protected by the ADA. This type of question is also prohibited.

Genetic Information Nondiscrimination Act of 2008 (GINA)
The GINA was signed into law in 2008 and became effective November 21, 2009. Title II applies to discrimination in employment. It prohibits discrimination and harassment based on genetic information. It also prohibits acquisition of genetic information by employers. This would include getting a family medical history. It also requires confidentiality of any genetic information obtained.

Improper Questions about Genetic Information
A. What is your family medical history?
This is a violation of GINA. An employer cannot ask you about your family medical history.

B. Have you taken any genetic tests to find out if you have a predisposition to any diseases? We need those results.
This is also a violation of GINA. It prohibits discrimination on the basis of genetic information.

Veteran Status

Vietnam Era Veterans' Readjustment Act (VEVRAA)
The affirmative action provisions of VEVRAA prohibit job discrimination and require federal contractors and subcontractors to take affirmative action to employ and advance in employment qualified Vietnam era veterans, special disabled veterans, recently separated veterans, and veterans who served on active duty during a war in a campaign or expedition for which a campaign badge has been authorized.

Uniformed Services Employment and Reemployment Rights Act (USERRA)
Military reservists and National Guard members called to active duty have rights and responsibilities under USERRA.

Veterans and State Laws
There is veterans preference in federal government jobs and in some states. Check your individual state to see what kind of veterans preference, if any, is required.

Improper Interview Questions about Veteran Status
A. Are you a disabled veteran?
Whether this is discrimination depends on the employer's intent. It is legal if the employer is asking this information in order to give veterans preference. It is illegal if the employer is asking this question in order to discriminate against a veteran. Veterans preference is usually part of the application process.

B. When was your military service?
It may be legal if the employer is trying to determine whether a veteran is protected by the Vietnam Era Veterans' Readjustment Act. It is illegal if the employer is asking the question in order to discriminate.

C. Did you serve in Vietnam?
In order to be protected by the Vietnam Era Veterans' Readjustment Act, it does not matter whether the veteran served in Vietnam, as long as the veteran was in military service during the Vietnam War era.

What if you are asked an illegal question in the interview?

The answer to this depends on how much you want the job. If you really want the job, you may want to give a light-hearted answer and say something like the following:

1. "I am sure you know you cannot ask that question, but I have nothing to hide. I have two children, ages three and four, and they go to daycare."

2. "Not that it is really your concern under federal law, but I do have two children, and their father takes them to daycare and I pick them up."

If you are personally affronted by the questions, you can tell the employer that you know your rights under the discrimination laws and that you are still interested in the position, but that you are going to refuse to answer the questions.

If you are really mad and now have no interest in the job, you could say that you know that they cannot ask these questions and you will be stopping by the regional office of the Equal Employment Opportunity Commission to file a complaint based on the protected category.

Chapter 6

The Waiting Game after the Interview

After the interview is over, the waiting game begins. There are some similarities between an interview and dating. You have to wait a few days to call or you will be considered too desperate.

Rule 29. Send a thank-you note.

Although it may seem old fashioned, you should still send a note or e-mail saying you enjoyed the interview and tell the employer that you are still very interested in the position. Perhaps you can ask a question to clarify something that came up in the interview. I prefer a mailed letter, but an e-mail is better than nothing. This seems very Emily Post, but when I get a letter from someone, which is not that often, I am usually very impressed by the gesture. If you are going to be reimbursed for expenses, you can use the thank-you letter as another way to recap the interview and say how interested you still are in the position. In addition, even if you don't get the position, you want the company to process your reimbursement check as soon as possible.

Rule 30. Give yourself a debriefing.

A debriefing is a way to evaluate the interview and make changes in future interviews. It is a good way to analyze what worked and what might need improvement. The answers to these questions will prepare you for your next interview. I like to put my debriefing in writing for future interviews. I don't like to make the same mistake twice.

A. Were you prepared enough?
Were you asked questions where more preparation would have helped you with the answer? Once I was asked what I knew about the employer and

except for a few facts gleaned from the internet, I had to admit that I didn't really know much. At that moment, I wished I had researched the company more thoroughly. Sometimes no amount of preparation would have helped you, but only you know that answer.

B. Were any mistakes made?
Did you say something you regretted? Did someone ask you something where your mind drew a blank? I have drawn a blank and no matter how hard I tried, I could not think of an answer. Finally I said that I could not answer and could we get to the next question. What could you do next time to avoid this kind of mistake?

C. What worked and what did not work?
Right after the interview, jot down some notes of your impressions of the interview before you forget. Ask yourself what worked and what did not work. Then you can ask yourself what you could have done differently. You might get the job, so at this point you really do not know what worked, but you can still have your hunches.

Rule 31. Determine if there are any red flags.
As part of the debriefing, you should list some of the red flags that may make working at this company unacceptable. You may have seen some things at this company that gave you pause about working there. In the excitement of going for an interview, do not overlook these red flags and listen to your gut. Here are some potential red flags:

A. I am not sure my management style is compatible with my new boss.
It is important that you and your new boss work well together. You may want to ask your prospective boss what his management style is and how he likes to work on projects.

B. I need to know how long my future boss intends to work before retiring.
Once I took a job and my boss almost immediately announced his retirement. I immediately started looking for a new job. After I left for that new job, my position was eliminated, so it is a good thing I was proactive. You might want to discretely ask your prospective employer what his future plans are.

C. I would like to know if they will train me and pay for me to go to conferences.

You may want to ask whether your prospective employer is willing to pay for you to attend a national conference each year and allow you to take training at the employer's expense. If this is important to you, it can be a red flag if the employer says no. Explain how important it is for you to keep current in your field.

D. I heard someone mention layoffs during my interview.

You might wonder if this is really true. If you have already been through a layoff, you probably want to avoid putting yourself in that position again.

Everyone's red flags will be different depending on their comfort levels on these issues. Of course, things will happen that are not foreseeable, but you want to know as much as you can about the current situation.

Rule 32. The employer is on its own timetable.

The interview may be the only thing on your mind. If you get the job, it totally changes your life, especially if the job is out of town. However, this job may be the last thing on the employer's mind. There may even be other positions that need to be filled before an offer is made on this particular job. You may get a call six months later saying that the position is not going to be filled and thanks for your patience. You may also get a call six months later saying that the company is now going to fill the position and it is wondering if you are still interested. The company has its own timetable, and there is nothing you can do about it. Here are some things that may be delaying a potential employer's decision.

A. There may be budgetary concerns before the employer can make an offer.

There may be budgetary issues, especially in this economy. The company may be trying to figure out if the duties associated with this position can be added to a current position so a new hire is not necessary. The employer may be intentionally delaying the hiring decision so that the salary has less impact on this year's budget.

B. The employer may be interviewing another candidate.

Even if the company offers the job to someone else, this may not mean you are totally out of the running. The employer may still find problems in the candidate's background that force it to withdraw the offer, or the other person may reject the offer. If that happens, your candidacy may be reconsidered.

I interviewed for a position in Colorado; I did not get it, and life went on. About a month later, I got a telephone call from the president, who asked if I was still interested since the top candidate declined the offer. He was very apologetic and gracious, saying that it was a very close call between the two top candidates and that he would pay for me to come out for a second interview. After I had the second interview, he offered me the job!

C. There may be dissension in the ranks.
The person who interviewed you may want to hire you, but he or she may need to convince the boss that you are a good fit. The boss may have another candidate in mind. These discussions can take time though, especially if there is resistance.

D. The employer may still be rethinking the position.
Even though the company has interviewed several candidates, it may still be thinking of a reorganization or merger of two positions, especially if there are budgetary concerns. It may ask itself whether anyone else can take on these duties so it doesn't have to hire a new employee.

E. The job may be on the back burner
The hiring officer may have left the company so there is no longer a champion for this position. Its importance may have waned because of the budget crunch, or the duties may have been absorbed by another employee. It may be revisited next year. Without a champion to keep the interest, it may stay on the back burner.

Rule 33. Don't be a nuisance if the employer does not call.

There are generally two schools of thought about calling back the employer and asking about the job selection. One is the person who will never call or do anything to find out whether he or she got the job. That person does not like to make those kinds of telephone calls and is willing to just wait. "If the company wants me, that is fine, but I am not going to go out of my way to find out."

The other extreme is the person who wants to call every day about the position. Don't be that person. That may cost you the job if you are too impatient. If you must call, call a week or so after human resources said it would make a decision. If HR said it would make a decision in a week, call in two weeks. These things usually take much longer than the original estimate. When you do call, ask whether a selection has been made. If not, ask if you can call in a week to see what the status is. If you are respectful and genuinely interested in the position, this can be a good thing. However, if you are a pest, that can work against you.

Some employers are rude and won't ever let you know the status of a position. Just follow up as much as you can without being too pushy. At some point, if you have not heard anything, you will have to assume you did not get the position and move on. When an employer does not answer calls or e-mails, you can read between the lines and presume he is not going to call you.

Rule 34. Do not get discouraged if you did not get the job.

Even if you don't get the job, the interview may help you nail the next interview. It is a good experience or dress rehearsal for the next one. I have learned something from every interview, and that nugget of experience always helps me in the next interview. Maybe it's the way I answered a question or the way I did not answer a question. Maybe it's a question I did not understand until it was too late. Maybe I was a smart aleck when I should have been serious. Maybe I should not have taken the interview so seriously. Maybe I fumbled a question. Maybe I learned something about the job that will help if I apply for a similar position in the future. There are many reasons why you might not have gotten the job, and many of them have nothing to do with you. Here are some possibilities:

A. Maybe the employer never filled the position.
Sometimes the employer will let you know and sometimes it won't. I have gotten calls six to nine months later asking me if I was still interested since the position had been frozen and now the company was trying to fill it.

B. Maybe there was an inside person.
Sometimes there is an inside candidate that the company wants to hire anyway, but it goes through the motions to make it look fair and legal. Sometimes there is a good inside employee, but the company wants to make sure he or she is the best candidate and it opens the position to outside candidates. The inside applicant's experience with the company usually gives him an advantage.

C. You had a negative check-off interview.
The company wants someone else, but because of your sex, age, race, expertise or education, the employer feels that it must interview you. The point of each question is to give you negative points so you don't get the job. The questions can sound almost accusatory.

I had one interviewer ask me if I had litigation experience at least five times. Litigation experience was not on the job notice. If it were, I would not have applied for the job. At one point, I got annoyed and said, "How many times do I have to tell you I don't have litigation experience?" I don't recommend mouthing off in the interview, but since I knew I wasn't going to get the job, I felt entitled to express my feelings. I got the impression that I was the most qualified person according to the job description and that I was getting a negative check-off interview so it would not have to consider me for the position.

Rule 35. Try to find out who did get the job.

After you have been told you did not get the job, ask the employer why. The best time to ask is when you are informed that you were not selected for the position. You could say something like, "I am very disappointed because I thought I was a good fit for the position. Can you tell me why I was not selected?" Some employers are afraid of giving out that information because they are afraid they might get sued. Usually the hiring supervisor or human resources representative will say something generic like "you were not the most qualified candidate." You might get lucky and get an honest answer. If it wasn't human resources who told you that you did not get the job, you might want to ask them if they know anything. "I really want to improve my interviewing skills, and if I got some feedback about the interview, I would really appreciate it."

You might also want to ask who was selected for the position. In the public sector in states like Florida, which has a strict government-in-the-sunshine law, the employer has to give you that information, including the salary of the new person. In addition, you might want to contact your references and see if they have any insight. The questions asked of your references may give you an idea about what they were looking for in a candidate.

Rule 36. Get back in the saddle.

As Frank Sinatra once sang, "Pick yourself up, dust yourself off, and get back in the race." You can't dwell on it. As indicated above, it is probably not about you. Personally, I find it is a hard transition. When you go to an interview, especially out of town, you imagine yourself living in this new town. You look around and see the good things that this area has to offer. I usually look at the apartments available and get a feel for the housing and shopping. I find that helps me to be enthusiastic in the interview. I envision myself in this job, in this town. Then after all that envisioning, it is a bit of a letdown to find I won't be moving after all.

Give yourself a pep talk. Remind yourself that you would not want a job if the company did not want you in the job. Just like dating, remind yourself that there are other fish in the sea. There are always other jobs. Let yourself think of the bad things about the job that you might have had misgivings about. Eventually, you will get a better job, and you will be glad you did not get this one.

Chapter 7. | You Got The Job!

You get the telephone call and the employer is ready to make you an offer. Here are some guidelines to help you through this process.

Rule 37. Get the employer to make the first offer, but never accept the employer's first offer.

This can be a little tricky. Always try to get the employer to make the first offer of salary. It can be very difficult, but it is usually a great advantage. The company may ask you what your salary requirements are. If the company won't give me a dollar amount, I try to ask a question. "How much is budgeted for this position?" or "What is the top of the range?"

Why is it so important for the employer to make the first offer? Here is an example. Let's say you are willing to take a position for $82,000. If the employer's first offer is $90,000, you are already $8,000 ahead and may be able to negotiate even more money. If you had asked for $82,000 or even $85,000, then that would be the most you could ever get. You would have left money on the table. However, if the company offers $75,000, you can still negotiate a higher figure to see if you can reach $82,000 as a compromise. Your counter-offer in this situation would probably be around $89,000.

As tempting as the employer's first offer may be, do not accept it right away. Always tell the employer that you need some time to sleep on it and you need to discuss it with your family. If possible, take the weekend to mull it over. That is a reasonable amount of time, and most employers will respect that. No matter how high the original offer is, chances are you can get a little more money or even something else. Remember that the company wants to hire you and you are the top candidate.

There usually is some wiggle room left on the table after a first offer is made. After you have had the weekend to think about it, go back the next day and ask for five thousand dollars more. Show that you have done some research based on your current salary, the salaries in the area, your added responsibilities, or the cost of living in that area. If the company wants you, it will probably go a little higher. If the company says it cannot go any higher, then you have to decide whether to accept the offer or not. There are exceptions to every rule. Once I got an offer that was so high that my brother-in-law said, "Mary, you better accept that offer before the company revokes it." I did.

Rule 38. Look at the full benefit picture before accepting an offer.

The job offer is much more than salary. Many candidates focus on the salary component and don't have a clear picture of the full benefit package. In addition to salary, there are many other benefits to consider. Usually there is not much negotiation involved if all the employees get the same benefits, although sometimes the executives get a separate benefit package.

A. Health Insurance

You need to know how much premium you will be paying. You should also find out how much premium is being subsidized by your employer. If you are single, it is more likely that this will be subsidized by the employer. If you have dependents, you need to find out how much premium you will pay and how much the company will contribute. This amount is likely to increase each year. Also ask when you are eligible to get the health insurance. Many companies require a sixty-day or ninety-day waiting period. If that is the case, you will need to make sure you have health insurance coverage until your new coverage kicks in.

B. Vacation and Sick Leave

Find out how much vacation and sick time you get. If you can negotiate an extra week of vacation, that is worth an extra two percent of salary. Many companies have personal time off (PTO), which combines traditional sick leave and vacation so that time is now either scheduled time off or unscheduled time off.

C. Retirement Benefits

Many new employees, especially young ones, are really not that concerned about retirement benefits, but they should be. Many companies are reducing or doing away with retirement benefits for new employees. Find out if you have a defined benefit or a defined contribution retirement plan.

With a defined benefit plan, you count the number of years worked times a multiplier such as 2 percent times the average of the five top years of salary or something similar to that. Many firefighters and police officers are in defined benefit programs. Defined benefit programs are less and less common, especially for new employees.

In a defined contribution plan, the plan and the employee contribute a certain percentage of salary and the individual employee manages the investment of the monies in the plan. These are called 401A plans in the public sector and 401K plans in the private sector. Since so many Americans lost so much money in 2008–2009, many employees are delaying retirement in the hopes that their retirement plans will recoup some of their losses.

Also find out what the vesting period is. If the vesting period is ten years and you leave after eight years, then you forfeit the employer's contribution and you will only get back what you contributed.

Your new employer may have a 457 Deferred Compensation Plan. This allows the employee to contribute money into the retirement plan pretax and manage the investments. Some employers have a matching plan, but this is getting less and less common because of budget shortfalls.

D. Exempt or Hourly?
You will want to know if you are a salaried employee or an hourly employee. This is also known as exempt or nonexempt in the Fair Labor Standards Act (FLSA). Nonexempt means that you get overtime for any hours worked over forty hours in any week. An exempt or salaried employee works a salary to get the job done and does not get overtime.

Rule 39. Ask yourself if you want something other than money.

Employers may not want to make increases to their salary offers, because it can affect other employees' salaries and can mean more money when raises are put into place. Here are some things you might want to request that do not affect the base salary.

A. Moving Expenses

If you will be moving, ask for moving expenses. This can give you some money now but won't affect your base salary. You can either ask for money for moving expenses, which is better for tax purposes, or for reimbursement of your actual moving expenses up to a certain amount.

B. A Different Title.

If the salary is sufficient, but you hate the position title, perhaps you can get it changed before you accept the offer.

C. Travel Expenses or Dues

Money is tight right now, so perhaps you can get a commitment to go to a national conference in your field or to pay your expenses to join a professional organization in your field.

D. Health Insurance Buyback Plan

See if the employer has a health insurance buyback plan if your health insurance is covered elsewhere. If you are covered by your spouse's insurance or old enough to be covered by Medicare, you can parlay that savings into an increase in your salary.

E. More Vacation.

Agree to keep the salary offered but ask for an extra week of vacation.

Try to think of something that you want that does not cost money but will make the offer more appealing to you. Since there are so many applicants for each position, you may not have that much leverage to be asking for much over the offered salary. The company's view may be that there are so many other applicants looking for jobs that it will go on to candidate two or three with its offer. It does not hurt to ask. Remember that it wants you for the position, not anyone else.

Rule 40: Ask yourself whether you really want this job.

You get the job offer and then decide that you are going to reject it. Once you have mulled over the job offer and written your lists of pros and cons, you have decided this job is not for you. You want to stay in your current job. Ask yourself why you were interested in the other job in the first place. Ask yourself why you are no longer interested. You want to make sure you made the right decision. As noted earlier, you never want to burn any bridges. You may have seller's remorse and decide at a later time that you made a mistake and you want to work for this company after all.

Once you make the decision, let the company know as soon as possible, and don't send an e-mail. Remember the episode of *Sex and the City* where one of Carrie's boyfriends breaks up with her with a post-it note? That was outrageous and inappropriate. If you are going to reject the offer, don't take the coward's way out. You must go in person or call the person you have been working with, not his or her assistant, and tell him or her that you are not going to take the position. Be prepared to give some good reasons. Here are some suggestions:

A. I really enjoyed the interview process, and I was very gratified that I was given this opportunity. However, after consulting with my family, I have decided to stay where I am so my children can finish their high school education in this town. (My father did this for me. I was entering my senior year in high school, and my father delayed a move to Pittsburgh so I could attend that last year of high school at the same school. That was a long time ago, but I am still grateful to him.)

B. As a result of the interview, I am looking at my current position in a new light. I realize now that I would be leaving some good projects that I would like to complete.

C. My father-in-law is ill, and we have decided to stay in this area so my wife can help with his treatment.

D. I have received two job offers this week, and after careful consideration, I have decided to go with the other offer. I really appreciate all the time and effort you gave me to introduce me to your company and your employees.

If you really don't have a good reason and just got cold feet about leaving your current job, just make up a good reason. You don't want your reason to make it look as though you wasted its time by spending time and effort on something that was never going to happen anyway. After you talk with someone, follow up with a nice letter explaining again why you are not taking the job, but emphasize how much you enjoyed meeting them and the time and effort they used to familiarize you with the company. Otherwise they may have second thoughts about reimbursing your travel expenses, so be sure to send that follow-up letter.

Can you leverage this job offer into a salary increase at your current employer? Whether you planned it or not, your boss may want to persuade you to stay after you tell him you have another job offer. If your boss asks you what it would take for you to stay, do not give an immediate response. As with the salary offer above, you need to think this through and ask family members the consequences of staying at your current job. Of course, money talks, at least to some extent. Again you need to ask yourself why you were dissatisfied with your current job in the first place. Is there something your boss can do, in addition to money, to encourage you to stay? If there is something that would improve your current job, let your boss know. You may have some bargaining chips if he or she really wants to keep you, so this is the time to ask for what you want.

This is now or never. Maybe you did not know how valued you were. Maybe there is a project you want to work on. Maybe there is a job title you have in mind. Maybe there is a course you want to take. If you stay, be very careful as to your boss's and your motivation. You do not want the whole thing to go sour next month when you have your first disagreement and you start daydreaming about the job that got away.

Will you take the job even if the salary package is less than you expected? If you really want the job, you need to ask yourself if you can live with the lower salary. I am assuming you have tried all the suggestions above, but that the employer has not budged. The company still wants you, but it is clear there is no more money to entice you to the position. What will you do? Here are some things to consider.

A. Have I learned everything I can at my current job?
You need to look at the pros and cons of your current job. If you truly have nothing more to learn at the old job, you may want to jump ship and try a new opportunity.

B. What are the real opportunities at the new job other than money?
Look at what your new job provides. Will there be better mentors, cutting-edge technology, or better working conditions? If not, you might want to stay put.

C. Does this fit in with my long-term goals?
First you need to know what your long-range plans are. If this new job fits into that plan, you might want to go forward. As they say, "opportunity only knocks once" and "opportunity often comes at an inopportune time." You have to consider whether this is a once-in-a-lifetime opportunity or one that you can still get a few years or months from now.

D. What does my family think? Do they support this?
What your family thinks is very important. With the problems of the economy, it is harder for families to make a move. It is a lot harder with the slow housing market to move to another geographic area and start over again.

E. Can I afford the lower salary? Do I need to get a second job?
Be realistic about how much money you need to live. If you need a second job, will that make the opportunities of the lower paying job less attractive? Will you have the time and energy to make the most of these new opportunities if you have to put in hours at a second job?

F. Is the experience invaluable?
If you do decide that you are going to take the job anyway, tell the company that you are so committed to the job that you have decided to accept the offer. Try to get a commitment as to when you will have your first performance review and whether you can be considered for a raise at that time.

Rule 41. Give proper notice.

The first question a new employer asks is how soon you can start. It is very exciting to get a new job offer, and it is tempting to start right away. However, resist that urge. It is very important to give your current employer sufficient notice. You need to give at least the minimum required by the company policy manual, whether it is two weeks or six weeks. However, sometimes an employer does not want your services once you inform your boss that you are leaving. I had one boss who viewed getting a job with someone else as a betrayal and did not even want to speak with me once I made the announcement that I was taking another job.

If you don't give proper notice, it can backfire on you. If you do not give proper notice to your current employer, your new boss may think you lack integrity. That is not a good way to start a new job. Your new boss may wonder what kind of notice you will give if and when you leave this job. Leaving without giving the proper notice can also mean that you did not leave in good standing and that could be reflected in any reference given by your old company.

Rule 42. Do not burn any bridges, and help with the transition.

Even if you did not like your old employer, be sure not to burn your bridges. Even though you don't like your current job now, you may want to come back to this job in the future. You just never know. It might feel good to go into your employer and say, "Take this job and shove it." Don't do it, because you may regret it later. Even if you never intend to work for this company again, you may need a reference from them in the future.

Help with the transition. Be sure to volunteer to help your old employer in the transition. Perhaps, during this transition, you can spend one day a week training your successor or wrapping up projects. Make a list of all the projects you are working on so there will be continuity after you leave. Helping your old employer makes you look good with your new employer. It knows that you have dedication and integrity so that when you leave its employ, you will do the same thing.

Rule 43. When you are the interviewer, remember what it was like to be interviewed.

Now that you have a new job, you may find that you are in the position of interviewing and hiring new employees. Now that you have gone through the process, try to have some empathy for the new applicants going through the process. Here are some suggestions:

A. Let applicants know in a timely fashion when they are no longer being considered for the job.

B. When you have interviewed someone, let them know when you will make the decision and try to be realistic.

C. If there is a delay in the selection process for some reason, let the applicants know.

D. Don't ask trick questions just to be funny.

F. If allowed, tell an applicant why he or she did not get the job.

G. Treat all applicants the way you would have liked to have been treated when you were interviewing.

H. After someone is hired, be a mentor and show the new applicant the ropes of his or her new job.

Chapter 8. | CONCLUSION: GETTING YOUR NEXT JOB

Finding a job is like parking; you have to be in the right place at the right time.

In the first seven chapters, I have given you some advice on how to interview and get the job that you want. Chapters 1 and 2 got you started and helped you to prepare for the interview. Chapters 3 and 4 got you through the interview and gave you some model answers for typical interview questions. Chapter 5 covered the laws of interviewing with a list of improper questions. Chapter 6 and Chapter 7 covered the aftermath of the interview with advice for negotiating salary and benefits. Along the way, I tried to give some examples from my own experience at interviews.

Readers often ask me about my favorite rules or the most important rules in my books. Here are what I consider the five top rules that are most essential to interviewing like a pro.

1. Getting a job is a full-time job.
Getting a job is hard work, and if you already have a job, then you now have two full-time jobs. This takes a daily routine. Get up at your regular time, get dressed for work, and start the job of getting a job. You need an action plan each day. It is easy to waste time and be lost on the computer. Mix it up and keep track of your time. Spend some time on the computer looking for leads. Then call contacts to see if you can meet at their offices to get advice about jobs in their fields. Call friends for lunch and see if they know of anything available. Don't stay in the house all day. Spend some time out in the field dressed for success and keep busy. Don't be afraid to ask people for help.

2. Be prepared.

Just like a good scout, you need to be prepared for every step of the interview process. Don't feel that you can wing it. Prepare in advance as much as you can. Your résumé needs to be error free and typo free. Even when you write your cover letter, you may need to research the company so your letter shows you understand its needs. Remember that your cover letter and résumé can be rejected in seconds. You need to say something that catches the eye of the reader. I like to say I am uniquely qualified for the position and explain why, using the job notice as my outline.

When you find out that you have an interview, you must start preparing. This includes knowing what you are going to wear as well as what you are going to say. You should be practicing in front of a mirror—or better yet, with a friend—and answering the questions that you think you will be asked. Don't forget to have an answer for that question that you don't want to answer. I am not asking you to memorize your answers. When you start giving answers that are memorized, it sounds phony. You need to think through your answers to crucial questions like "Why do you want to leave your current job?" or "Why were you fired from your last job?" or "What would your current boss say about your performance?" Be prepared and be honest. If you had some problems in a previous job, you need to be upfront about it, because the employer will probably get this information from another source, such as a background check, and you want the employer to hear your version first.

3. Give yourself a debriefing after each interview.

Ask yourself a few questions to see if you can determine why you did not get the job. You can usually learn something from each interview that will help you in the next one. Sometimes you will never know what went wrong, but usually there is at least one question that doesn't go well or a silence that seems awkward or a random comment that gives you a clue. Of course, the reason you did not get the job might not have anything to do with you. For example, the employer might have picked someone it preferred even before the interviewing began. Here are some questions to consider:

A. How did I answer the interview questions?

B. How can I improve my answers?

C. Why didn't I get the job? Was it me?

D. When did it go wrong? Or was it a good interview?

E. Did they see some weaknesses? How can I explain this or make it a strength?

4. Don't get discouraged.

When you get that thanks-but-no-thanks letter, it is important not to get discouraged. You may have really wanted this job and already imagined yourself living in this new town and even had your new office decorated in your head. You are allowed some disappointment, but try to think positively. Like the Frank Sinatra song, you do have to "pick yourself up and get back in the game." This is why you don't stop your job search when you get your first good interview. Even if this is your dream job, you still have to keep going until you receive an offer letter and have accepted it. Even that may not be enough, because most employers give you a conditional letter so they can do a background check. Don't stop your job search or quit your current job until you get a final offer, not a conditional offer. If you feel rejected, you have to give yourself a pep talk and start the process all over again. You need to project a confident demeanor. If you don't feel that confident, fake it for a while until you do feel confident again. Remember, the reason you did not get the job might not have had anything to do with you. Some people wallow in self pity; don't be one of those people. It does not help you get the job.

5. Don't accept the first offer.

When you finally get that offer, don't be overanxious and accept it right away. Always give yourself some time to analyze the offer and ask questions. Always ask for some time to sleep on it and discuss it with your family. Remember that this employer has chosen you for this position, and there is probably some money still on the table. Do your homework and determine comparable salaries in the geographic area. You need to look at the complete offer package. What are the benefits offered, and is there anything else you may want other than money? Give the employer a counteroffer based on your research. If you are reluctant to ask for more money, remember that the salary you negotiate today will be the basis for raises and promotions in the future. Even a thousand-dollar increase can have an impact on your future salary. Don't stop your job search or quit your current job until you get a final offer, not a conditional offer.

Remember, getting a job is like parking: you have to be in the right place at the right time. If you follow these rules, you can interview like a pro.

APPENDIX A:
Dos and Don'ts of Interviewing

Don't

1. Appear disinterested
2. Be arrogant
3. Have a sense of entitlement
4. Use your cell phone
5. Text
6. Speak negatively about your boss
7. Recite poetry
8. File your nails
9. Give weird references like Harry Potter or Dungeons and Dragons
10. Wear flip-flops
11. Look at the ceiling during the interview
12. Bring your mother or relative to the interview
13. Swear
14. Ask the interviewer for a drink or date
15. Ask how long the interview will take
16. Take charge; it's the company's interview
17. Breach confidentiality
18. Say you have no interests or hobbies
19. Be vague in your answers
20. Get flustered
21. Use a weird tag name on your e-mail
22. Drop names
23. Bring food to the interview
24. Be too casual
25. Be evasive
26. Dress inappropriately with tight clothes, cleavage, or too much jewelry

Do

1. Be interested
2. Be respectful
3. Explain your situation without blaming anyone
4. Dress appropriately
5. Look the interviewer(s) in the eye
6. Answer the questions as best as you can
7. Ask for an explanation if you don't understand a question
8. Show that you have interests and hobbies other than your job
9. Be discrete with confidential information
10. Be diplomatic
11. Be enthusiastic
12. Be calm, cool, and collected
13. Smile
14. Shake hands
15. Be polite
16. Think before speaking
17. Be a good listener
18. Be personable
19. Be creative
20. Be ethical
21. Be honest
22. Be patient
23. Have a sense of humor
24. Be sincere
25. Be attentive
26. Be yourself
27. Enjoy the interview

APPENDIX B:
Glossary of Terms

Affirmative Action means positive steps taken to increase the representation of women and minorities in employment and education.

Action Verbs that describe your experience, qualifications, and skills should be used in your résumé instead of the words *be* or *do*.

The **Age Discrimination in Employment Act of 1967** prohibits discrimination on the basis of age against employees forty years of age or older.

The **Americans with Disabilities Act (ADA)** prohibits discrimination against those with disabilities who can perform the duties of the position with or without reasonable accommodation.

An **Application for Employment** is usually required before or after an interview. Although it is much of the same information that is already found on your résumé, the employer needs that information in a set format. It is absolutely essential that this information is accurate. If there are discrepancies, these are grounds for dismissal even after if you are hired.

Background Checks are used by employers to verify the information you gave on the application, such as college degrees, previous employment, references, court records, criminal records, and sometimes credit history. You need to read the application carefully, because you are giving permission to verify this information when you sign.

A **Behavioral Interview of** is the type of interview where the applicant's experience is thought to be predictive of future experience. A sample question would be, "Give me an example of a situation where there was conflict and you were able to resolve it."

Benefits are offered in addition to salary and include things like vacations, sick leave, life insurance, medical insurance, retirement and pension plans, tuition remission, child care, and stock options.

Bona Fide Occupational Qualification (BFOQ) is a term used in labor law. If sex, national origin, religion or age is a valid requirement for a job, it is a BFOQ. Race can never be a BFOQ. This is very strictly construed by the courts, and there are very few types of jobs where one of these protected categories can be a BFOQ. Examples are a female bikini model, a female restroom attendant, a male sperm donor, and an Asian actress.

Branding has become a popular buzz word. Your special brand can set you apart from other applicants.

Business Necessity is a defense to a discrimination complaint. An employer must show that a practice or rule is essential to the safety and efficiency of the business. Business necessity is used synonymously with the term *job related.*

Buzz Words are words that are used in your field and are also called jargon.

A **Career Objective** can be included in your résumé, usually at the top. It can customize your résumé and clarify your job search.

A **Case Scenario Review Interview** is a type of interview that gives the applicant an exercise to complete, such as a case study or fact pattern with questions.

A **Chronological Résumé** lists your previous jobs in reverse chronological order (with your most recent job first) as opposed to listing positions by skills or job functions.

The **Civil Rights Act of 1866,** known as Section 1981 of the Civil Rights Act, was the first major antidiscrimination employment statute. This act prohibits employment discrimination based on race and color. This act has been interpreted by the Supreme Court to protect all ethnic groups.

The **Civil Rights Act of 1871,** known as Section 1983 of the Civil Rights Act, provides a way for individuals to redress violations of federally protected rights and prohibits discrimination on the basis of race, color, national origin, sex, and religion.

A **Cold Call** is contacting an employer who does not have any position openings, usually through a cover letter. You should customize the letter to this employer rather than using a form letter, which will probably be thrown in the trash.

Comparable Worth is a theory of equal pay for comparable positions even though they are not equal in skill, effort, and responsibility.

Compensatory Damages pay discrimination victims for out-of-pocket expenses, such as costs associated with a job search or medical expenses, and pay them for any emotional harm suffered, such as mental anguish, inconvenience, or loss of enjoyment of life. There are limits on the amount of compensatory and punitive damages one person can recover, depending on the size of the employer. For an employer with fifteen to one hundred employees, it is $50,000. For an employer with five hundred or more employees, the cap is $300,000.

Corporate Culture is the collection of values and norms shared by people and groups in an organization that control the way they interact with each other. The corporate cultures of Microsoft and Google are known to be casual and unstructured, while the corporate culture of a large bank or law firm is likely to be more structured and formal.

A **Counteroffer** is a technique used in salary negotiations. The offer on the table is rejected and another offer is made.

A **Cover Letter** should always accompany a résumé when applying for a job. It pinpoints the experiences on your résumé that are relevant to the job and add other factors, such as your personality or integrity, that are not on your résumé. The employer is unlikely to read your résumé if your cover letter is not interesting.

A **Curriculum Vitae,** known as a CV, is often used in academia. It is a longer, more-detailed version of a résumé that includes publications and committee work. It is most commonly used in academia, but other fields are now using it as well.

Degrees should not be included on your résumé unless you actually completed them. If you did not graduate, just put that you attended with how many credits or years. Employers do check this and may ask for transcripts.

A **Declining Letter** is a letter sent to an employer after an employer has made a job offer and you have decided to decline. It needs to be diplomatic in case you want to work for the employer later on.

De Minimis is Latin for "minimal." For example, accommodation of religious discrimination is required, but only if it does not create an undue hardship. The standard for undue hardship is *de minimis*.

A **Disability** is an impairment that substantially limits one or more major life activities, a record of such an impairment, or being regarded as having such an impairment.

Discrimination is treating a person adversely because of race, religion, color, disability, gender, age, or national origin.

Disparate Impact describes a rule that is neutral on its face but has an adverse impact on a protected group. There can be disparate treatment discrimination even if there is no intent.

Disparate Treatment is when an employer intentionally treats applicants and employees differently because of race, color, sex, religion, national origin, age, sexual orientation, or disability.

Diversity acknowledges differences in culture and experience. This can include age, ethnicity, class, gender, race, sexual orientation, religion, geographical location, income, marital status, and work experience.

An **Electronic Résumé** is sent via e-mail to job boards or directly to the employer's web page. It is important to have key words on the résumé, because it may be filtered to determine qualified applicants.

An **Elevator Speech** is a short speech that you could give on an elevator ride that tells in thirty seconds or less who you are, what you can offer, and what you are looking for in a job. These are used to network, during job interviews, at job fairs—anywhere you are talking to someone about your job prospects.

The **Equal Employment Opportunity Commission** is a federal agency administering Title VII of the Civil Rights Act, Age Discrimination in Employment Act, and Genetic Information Nondiscrimination Act of 2008.

The **Equal Pay Act of 1967** prohibits compensation inequities based on sex. Men and women similarly situated with the same experience, education level, and expertise should be making the same salary.

The **Family Medical Leave Act** provides eligible employees up to twelve weeks of unpaid leave per year, and their jobs are protected during that time period if they are absent for the following reasons: 1) for the birth and care of the newborn child of an employee, 2) for placement with the employee of a child for adoption or foster care, 3) to care for an immediate family member (spouse, child, or parent) with a serious health condition, or 4) to take medical leave when the employee is unable to work because of a serious health condition.

Gaps are those periods of time when an applicant is not employed. Whether they occur because you were going to school, raising children, or doing volunteer work, these gaps need to be explained.

The **Genetic Information Nondiscrimination Act of 2008** prohibits discrimination against employees or applicants because of genetic information. Genetic information cannot be used in any employment decision.

A **Group Interview** is an interview where several candidates are in the same group. For example, they may each make a presentation and then take questions from the various constituencies. Traditionally, candidates do not interact with each other, but in this type of interview, they are all at the same venue rather than having separate interviews.

The **Immigration Reform and Control Act (IRCA)** prohibits employers from knowingly hiring, recruiting, or referring an alien who is unauthorized to work.

Inclusion is emphasizing and creating a supportive environment for those in a protected class, often used with diversity.

Intentional Discrimination is knowingly and purposefully treating members of a protected group differently from other employees and applicants because they are members of a protected group. This is synonymous with the term *disparate treatment*.

Internships are a good way to get on-the job experience through a college credit program or a summer program (with or without pay). Mentorship is usually provided, and such programs are a good way to break into a particular field or particular company. They help provide the bridge between education and work by providing experience in the field.

An **Interview** is a formal meeting during which an employer tries to determine whether an applicant is suitable for a job while the applicant tries to find out more about the position and the company.

Job-Related Skills are used in only one job or industry. For example, an x-ray technician has skills running an x-ray machine that are not transferable to another job.

A **Key-Word Résumé** is a résumé that is able to be scanned. It contains key words from the job description and position announcement so it will be picked up by the computers scanning for particular key words in résumés.

The **Lily Ledbetter Fair Pay Act** amends the Civil Rights Act of 1964 so that the 180-day statute of limitations for filing an equal-pay lawsuit regarding pay discrimination resets with each discriminatory paycheck. This allows someone who did not know of the discrimination for many years to still file a complaint after she finds out.

LinkedIn (www.linkedin.com) is a Facebook for professionals. This is a way to meet up with former colleagues and join groups on job hunting and in your field.

Liquidated Damages may be awarded to punish an especially malicious or reckless act of discrimination. The amount of liquidated damages that may be awarded is equal to the amount of back pay awarded to the victim.

Minorities include African Americans, Hispanics, and other protected groups. Minorities include those covered by race and national origin discrimination, and the groups may overlap.

National Origin describes a person's ancestry or birthplace or the physical, cultural, or linguistic characteristics of a group. National origin discrimination is prohibited by Title VII of the Civil Rights Act of 1964.

A **Negative Check-Off Interview** is an interview with the intent of giving the applicant negative points so he or she does not get the job. This approach is often used when the interviewee is protected by sex, race, or national origin discrimination laws or has the education or experience for the job. The employer asks specific questions so that it can give negative scores so the person interviewed won't get the job.

Negotiating against Yourself occurs when you make another offer when there already is an offer on the table. If you do not wait for a counteroffer, you will be negotiating against yourself. For example, you offer $5000, and then you offer $10,000 after you do not get a response to the first offer. If you had asked for a counteroffer instead, the other party might have countered with $7500, and you would have gained $2500. Never make two offers in a row. Always ask for a counteroffer.

Networking is a way to broaden your contacts by attending social, business, and professional functions. Networking with friends and acquaintances can help you get leads, advice or mentoring. Internet networks like LinkedIn (www. linkedin. com) provide a system of potential contacts.

Nontraditional Careers are careers that were traditionally one-gender jobs. For example, nursing used to be nontraditional for men, and construction is still generally a nontraditional career for women.

An **Offer of Employment** is an offer that spells out the terms of employment, such as salary, benefits, pensions, and other working conditions. Don't quit your current job until you get the offer in writing and have accepted it. Make sure it is not a conditional offer, which means the company is checking out your background or requires a drug test before giving you a final offer.

Overqualified is a term used as an excuse not to hire someone who has a lot of experience or education or is highly paid. However, saying someone is overqualified may be grounds for a discrimination complaint.

A **Panel Interview** is an interview with several people who will interact with an open position in different ways. For example, there may be a representative from human resources, a department head, a member of the union, a member of the public, and various committee members on a panel. Each person will have a different interest in the position. Usually, each person gets to ask one question. This can be a screening interview after which top applicants will interview with someone else, such as the supervisor of the position.

Passive Job Seekers are those not actively seeking work. Some employers seek out passive job seekers since they are supposedly happily employed and may be an asset to the company if persuaded to jump ship.

A **Phone Interview** is usually used to screen employees to determine who will be invited for a face-to-face interview. With increased financial concerns, phone interviews will be used more often.

Personnel Time Off (PTO) combines the old concepts of sick leave and vacation leave. When you take time off whether it is for illness or for vacation, it is counted as scheduled time off or unscheduled time off.

The **Pregnancy Discrimination Act** prohibits an employer from refusing to hire a pregnant woman because of her pregnancy, because of a pregnancy-related condition, or because of the prejudices of co-workers, clients, or customers. If a pregnant woman has complications, she may also be covered by the Americans with Disabilities Act.

A **Pretext** is an excuse used by an employer to discriminate against an employee or potential employee. An employer must prove that the business necessity reasons offered are the real reasons for the discrimination and not a pretext for discrimination.

A **Protected Class or Category** cannot be used as a basis for discrimination. Protected categories include race, religion, sex, national origin, disability, sexual orientation, and age.

Punitive Damages may be awarded to punish an employer who has committed an especially malicious or reckless act of discrimination. There are limits on the amount of compensatory and punitive damages one person can recover, depending on the size of the employer. For an employer with fifteen to one hundred employees, it is $50,000. For an employer with five hundred or more employees, the cap is $300,000

Race Discrimination is discriminating against someone because of his or her race. Race discrimination is prohibited by Title VII of the Civil Rights Act of 1964.

Racial Harassment includes racist comments or ethnic slurs that create a hostile environment or interfere with an employee's job performance. Racial harassment is prohibited by Title VII of the Civil Rights Act of 1964.

Reasonable Accommodation is required of employers under the Americans with Disabilities Act for employees who can perform the duties of the job with such accommodation without creating an undue hardship on the employer. Reasonable accommodation could include job restructuring, modifying the work schedule, modifying equipment, making existing facilities accessible, or providing an interpreter or reader. An employer must accommodate an employer's religious beliefs if this is not an undue hardship. *Reasonable* means that the accommodation is feasible or plausible.

References are people who know you and can tell your future employer information about your experience, abilities, and character. Be sure to ask before you list someone as a reference. Let your references know about a job interview before they are called.

Religious Discrimination is prohibited by Title VII of the Civil Rights Act of 1964. The EEOC defines religion as "all aspects of religious observance and practice, as well as belief, unless the employer demonstrates that he is unable to reasonably accommodate to an employee's or prospective employee's religious observance without undue hardship on the conduct of the employer's business."

A **Résumé** is a very important tool for getting an interview. It summarizes your job experience, education, skills, and accomplishments.

Retaliation is when an adverse personnel action is taken because an employee filed a discrimination complaint or opposed an employer's practice.

Sexual Harassment can include unwelcome sexual advances and requests for sexual favors. It is unlawful to harass a person (an applicant or employee) because of that person's sex. Harassment does not have to be of a sexual nature, however, and can include offensive remarks about a person's sex. Both the victim and the harasser can be either a woman or a man, and the victim and harasser can be the same sex.

Sexual Orientation Discrimination is treating someone differently from others on the basis of his or her sexual orientation. In other words, treating a homosexual or bisexual person differently from a heterosexual person is sexual orientation discrimination.

A **Screening Interview** is a preliminary interview, often by phone, to determine if you will be one of the final candidates for the position. Sometimes it is carried out by the human resources department to determine if you meet the criteria for the position. Often, the supervisor for this position is not present at this screening or preliminary interview but may be in charge of the second interview.

A **Stress Interview** is a type of interview designed to determine how an applicant reacts under stress. The interviewer may be antagonistic or bullying just to see how the applicant reacts under this type of pressure. The interviewer may arrive late or give the applicant the silent treatment just to see his or her reaction. This type of interview was used primarily for sales positions and is not that common anymore.

Testing may be part of the interview process. After a traditional interview, you may be asked to take a test, such as a personality, aptitude, or drug test. If you find any of these tests offensive, you have the opportunity to refuse, but, of course, you won't get the job.

Thank-You Letters are recommended for applicants to send after their interviews to show their continued interest in a position.

Title VI of the Civil Rights Act prohibits discrimination on the basis of race, color, sex, religion, and national origin in programs that get federal funding.

Title VII of the Civil Rights Act of 1964 prohibits discrimination on the basis of race, color, sex, religion, and national origin.

Title IX of the Education Amendments Act of 1972 prohibits sex discrimination in schools.

Transferable Skills are skills like communication, organization, problem solving, teamwork, and multi-tasking that can be transferred from one job to another field or industry.

Text Telephone (TTY) and Telecommunication Device for the Deaf (TDD) are often used interchangeably. TTY is the more widely accepted term since the device is not only used by the deaf. A TTY is a special device that lets people who are deaf, hard of hearing or speech-impaired use the telephone by allowing them to type messages back and forth, instead of talking and listening. The device is required at both ends of the call in order for the parties to communicate. If one does not have a TTY device, it is is possible to make a call with a Telecommunication Relay Service (TRS). The TRS is available in all fifty states to allow people with hearing or speech disabilities to make calls. The TRS system uses Communication Assistants (CA's) to facilitate the calls. The technology uses the TYY system and the CA serves as a link to relay the call.

Undue Hardship for Disability Under the Americans with Disabilities Act (ADA) means significant difficulty or expense and focuses on the resources and circumstances of the employer in relation to the cost or difficulty of providing a specific accommodation. If it is too expensive or disrupts the nature or operation of the business, then it is undue hardship. This assessment is done on a case-by-case basis by the employer. Large corporations are held to a higher standard than very small businesses. This is a different standard than for religious accommodation under Title VII.

Undue Hardship for Religious Accommodation under Title VII means that accommodation of an employee's religion cannot pose more than a *de minimis* cost or burden. This is a much lower standard for an employer to meet than undue hardship under the Americans with Disabilities Act. Factors the employer can consider are the type of workplace, the nature of the employee's duties, the cost of the accommodation, and the number of employees needing the accommodation. Some examples are shift swaps for religious observance, making an exception to dress codes, and use of the work facility for religious observance.

A **Vietnam-Era Veteran** is a veteran of any of the armed services from August 5, 1964 to May 7, 1975.

Veterans Preference is given in many federal jobs; usually five extra points are given for veterans and ten extra points for veterans who have received the Purple Heart. Some states also have veterans preference for state jobs.

APPENDIX C:
Federal Laws Prohibiting Discrimination

Here is a list of federal laws by category:

1. Race
A. Title VII of the Civil Rights Act of 1964
B. Civil Rights Act of 1886 (Section 1981)
C. Civil Rights Act of 1871 (Section 1983)
D. Title VI of the Civil Rights Act of 1964
E. Executive Order 11246

2. Color
A. Title VII of the Civil Rights Act of 1964
B. Civil Rights Act of 1871 (Section 1983)
C. Executive Order 11246 of 1965

3. National Origin
A. Title VII of the Civil Rights Act of 1964.
B. Title VI of the Civil Rights Act of 1964
C. Civil Rights Act of 1871 (1983)
D. Executive Order 11246
E. Immigration and Reform Act of 1986

4. Sex
A. Title VII of the Civil Rights Act of 1964
B. Civil Rights Act of 1871 (Section 1983)
C. Equal Pay Act of 1963
D. Title IX of the Education Amendments of 1972
E. Executive Order 11246
F. Pregnancy Discrimination Act of 1978
G. Family Medical Leave Act
H. Americans with Disabilities Act
I. Lily Ledbetter Fair Pay Act
J. Proposed Legislation: Paycheck Fairness Act

K. Proposed Legislation: Employment Nondiscrimination Act (ENDA)

5. Religion
A. Title VII of the Civil Rights Act of 1964
B. Executive Order 11246
C. Title VI of the Civil Rights Act of 1964

6. Age
A. Age Discrimination in Employment Act of 1967
B. Age and State Laws
C. Proposed Legislation: Protecting Older Workers Against Discrimination Act

7. Disability
A. Americans with Disabilities Act
B. Family Medical Leave Act
C. Genetic Information Discrimination Act

8. Veteran
A. Vietnam Era Veterans Readjustment Act:
B. Uniformed Services Employment and Reemployment Rights Act (USERRA)
C. Veterans and State Laws

Here is a brief description of several of the most important laws prohibiting discrimination:

A. Title VII of the Civil Rights Act
1. Discrimination Prohibited
Race
Color
Sex
Religion
National Origin

2. Coverage
Private employers with fifteen or more employees
State and local governments
Federal executive agencies
Labor unions

3. Enforcement Agency
Equal Employment Opportunity Commission (EEOC)
Contact the EEOC at 1-800-669-4000, visit their website at www. eeoc. gov, or contact a local office in your state.

4. Remedies
Back pay and interest
Front pay
Injunctions
Affirmative Action
Reinstatement
Hiring
Promotion
Seniority
Attorneys' fees and costs

B. Title VI of the Civil Rights Act of 1964.
1. Discrimination Prohibited
Race
Color
National Origin

2. Coverage:
Programs and activities that receive federal financial aid

3. Enforcement Agency
US Department of Justice
Call 888-848-5306, 202-307-222 (voice), or 202-307-2678(TDD), or visit their website at http://www. justice. gov/crt

4. Remedies
Cutoff of federal funds
Affirmative Action

C. Civil Rights Act of 1886 (Section 1981)
1. Discrimination Prohibited
Race, National Origin

2. Coverage:
Private Employers
State and local governments

3. Enforcement Agency
US Department of Justice
Call 888-848-5306, 202-307-222 (voice), or 202-307-2678(TDD), or visit their website at http://www. justice. gov/crt

4. Remedies
Compensatory damages
Punitive damages
Back pay and interest
Reinstatement
Hiring
Promotion
Affirmative Action

D. Race and the Civil Rights Act of 1871 (Section 1983)
This law was passed in 1871 and is known as Section 1983. This act prohibits intentional discrimination if it deprives a person of Constitutional Rights. State and local governments, state and local officials, and private employers involved in governmental functions are covered by this law, and it is also enforced by the US Department of Justice.
1. Discrimination Prohibited
Race
Color
Sex
National Origin
Religion

2. Coverage
State and local governments
State and local officials
Private employers involved in governmental functions

3. Enforcement Agency
US Department of Justice
Call 888-848-5306, 202-307-222 (voice), or 202-307-2678(TDD), or visit their website at http://www. justice. gov/crt

4. Remedies
Compensatory damages
Punitive damages

Back pay and interest
Reinstatement
Hiring
Promotion
Affirmative Action
Attorneys' fees and costs

E. Executive Order 11246 of 1965
1. Discrimination Prohibited
Race
Color
Sex
Religion
National Origin

2. Coverage
Organizations with $10,000 in federal contractors: Nondiscrimination
Organizations with $50,000 in federal contracts: Written Affirmative Action Plan

3. Enforcement Agency
Office of Federal Contract Compliance (OFCCP)
US Department of Labor

4. Remedies
Back pay and interest
Hiring
Promotion
Reinstatement
Goals and Timetables
Termination of current federal contracts
Debarment from future contracts

F. Immigration Reform and Control Act of 1986
1. Discrimination Prohibited
National Origin
Citizenship status—an employer may not treat legal aliens intending to become citizens differently from citizens.

2. Coverage
All employers with four or more employees

3. Enforcement Agency
US Department of Justice, Civil Rights Division
Call the Office of Special Counsel hotline at 1-800-255-8155 (toll free) or
1-800-362-2735 (TDD) or visit their website at http://www. justice. gov/crt/
osc/pdf/publications/Employer_IRCA. pdf

4. Remedies
Reinstatement
Back pay
Civil penalties of up to $1000 per person for the first offense
Civil penalties of up to $2000 per person for each subsequent offense

G. Equal Pay Act of 1963
1. Discrimination Prohibited
Pay inequities based on sex

2. Coverage
Private employers with two or more employees
State and local governments
Labor Unions

3. Enforcement Agency:
Equal Employment Opportunity Commission (EEOC)
Contact the EEOC at 1-800-669-4000, visit their website at www. eeoc. gov,
or contact a local office in your state.

4. Remedies
Back pay (double backpay if employer was willful)
Front pay
Attorneys' Fees
Injunctions

H. Title IX of Education Amendments of 1972
1. Discrimination Prohibited
Sex discrimination in education (both males and females)

2. Coverage
Any educational program or activity receiving federal funds

3. Enforcement
US Department of Education and US Department of Justice
Call 800-421-3481 or 877-521-2172 (TDD), fax 202-453-6012, or e-mail
OCR@ed. gov.
To file a Title IX complaint, visit this website: http://www2. ed. gov/about/
offices/list/ocr/complaintintro. html

4. Remedies:
Cutoff of federal funds

I. Pregnancy Discrimination Act of 1978
1. Discrimination
Pregnancy discrimination

2. Coverage
Private employers with fifteen or more employees
State and local governments
Federal executive agencies
Labor unions
Employment agencies

3. Enforcement Agency
Equal Employment Opportunity Commission (EEOC)
Contact the EEOC at 1-800-669-4000, visit their website at www. eeoc. gov,
or contact a local office in your state.

4. Remedies
Back pay and interest
Front pay
Reinstatement
Hiring
Promotion
Attorneys' fees and costs

J. Lily Ledbetter Fair Pay Act
1. Discrimination Prohibited
Compensation discrimination under Title VII, ADEA, and ADA

2. Coverage
Renews the statute of limitations for pay discrimination cases under Title VII
and ADEA each time a paycheck is received. A complainant may file a complaint

within 180 days of one of the following: a) when a discriminatory compensation decision or other discriminatory practice affecting compensation is adopted; b) when the individual becomes subject to a discriminatory compensation decision or other discriminatory practice affecting compensation; or c) when the individual's compensation is affected by the application of a discriminatory compensation decision or other discriminatory practice, including each time the individual receives compensation that is based in whole or part on such a compensation decision or other practice.

3. Enforcement Agency
Equal Employment Opportunity Commission (EEOC)
Contact the EEOC at 1-800-669-4000, visit their website at www. eeoc. gov, or contact a local office in your state.

4. Remedies
Back Pay

K. Sex and the Proposed Paycheck Fairness Act
The proposed Paycheck Fairness Act would amend the Equal Pay Act.
1. Discrimination Prohibited
Sex Discrimination in the payment of wages

2. Coverage
Amends the portion of the Fair Labor Standards Act of 1938 (FLSA) known as the Equal Pay Act to revise remedies for enforcement of sex discrimination in the payment of wages; revises prohibition against employer retaliation for employee complaints; amends Civil Rights Act of 1964 to require the EEOC to collect pay information data regarding the sex, race, and national origin of employees for use in the enforcement of federal laws prohibiting pay discrimination.

3. Enforcement Agency
EEOC and OFCCP Office of the Department of Labor

4. Remedies
Employers who violate sex discrimination prohibitions are liable in a civil action for either compensatory or punitive damages.

L. Sex and the Proposed Employment Nondiscrimination Act (ENDA)
1. Discrimination Prohibited
This proposed legislation would prohibit discrimination on the basis of sexual orientation and gender identity.

2. Coverage
Employers, employment agencies, labor organizations

3. Enforcement Agency
Equal Employment Opportunity Commission (EEOC)

4. Remedies
Same remedies as Title VII

M. Age Discrimination in Employment Act of 1967
1. Discrimination Prohibited
Age discrimination for employees and applicants forty and over

2. Coverage:
Private employers with twenty or more employees
State and local governments
Federal executive agencies
Unions
Employment agencies

3. Enforcement Agency
Equal Employment Opportunity Commission (EEOC)
Contact the EEOC at 1-800-669-4000, visit their website at www. eeoc. gov, or contact a local office in your state.

4. Remedies
Back pay
Double back pay (called compensatory) if employer was willful
Front Pay
Reinstatement
Injunctions
Attorneys' fees and costs

N. Age and the Proposed Protecting Older Workers Against Discrimination Act
This legislation overrules the Gross v. FBL Financial Services Case, 129 S. Ct. 2343. In the Gross case, the plaintiff was fifty-three years old, and he was

demoted and his duties were transferred to an employee in her forties. Gross then filed a claim under the Age Discrimination in Employment Act. At trial, the jury was instructed that if age was a motivating factor in the demotion, the verdict should be for the plaintiff. The plaintiff won, but FBL appealed based on the jury instruction. The Supreme Court held in a 5-4 decision that a mixed-motive jury instruction is not available to the plaintiff in an ADEA case. The proposed legislation would have the same mixed-motive protection that exists under Title VII. The latest version was introduced in the Senate on March 13, 2012.

O. Americans with Disabilities Act (ADA)
1. Discrimination Prohibited
Discrimination against people with disabilities
A qualified individual with a disability means an individual who, with or without reasonable accommodation, can perform the essential functions of the employment position.
An applicant or employee is disabled if he or she has
- physical or mental impairment that substantially limits one or more major life activities, such as breathing, hearing, or walking.
- a record of such impairment, or
- is regarded as having such an impairment.

2. Coverage
Employment, transportation, public accommodations, communications and governmental entities

3. Enforcement
Equal Employment Opportunity Commission (EEOC)
Department of Transportation, (DOT)
Federal Communications Commission (FCC),
Department of Justice (DOJ),
Department of Labor (DOL) Office of Federal Contract Compliance Programs (OFCCP) has coordinating authority under employment provisions of the ADA.
Department of Labor (DOL), Civil Rights Center has authority of enforcing labor and workplace related practices of state and local governments and other public entities.

4. Remedies
Back pay
Compensatory damages
Attorneys' fees
Punitive damages
Front pay
Injunctive relief

P. The Family Medical Leave Act (FMLA)
1. Discrimination Prohibited
Employer must provide eligible employees up to twelve weeks of unpaid leave for serious medical conditions.

2. Coverage
Employers with fifty employees in a seventy-five mile radius.

3. Enforcement Agency
The Wage and Hour Division of the US Department of Labor
Call 1-866-4USWAGE (1-866-487-9243)
To file a complaint, visit their website: http://www. dol. gov/compliance/laws/comp-fmla. htme

4. Remedies
Back pay
Actual damages
Liquidated damages
Attorneys' fees
Injunctive relief

Q. Vietnam Era Veterans' Readjustment Act of 1974
1. Discrimination prohibited
Disabled veterans
Vietnam-Era Veterans (August 5, 1964 to May 7, 1975)

2. Coverage
Federal contractors and subcontractors
Federal agencies

3. Enforcement Agency
Office of Federal Contract Compliance Programs (US Department of Labor)
Call 1-866-4-USA-DOL (1-866-487-2365) (1-866- 487-2365), or 1-800-397-6251. TTY: 1-877-889-5627. E-mail: OFCCP-Public@dol. gov
To file a complaint, visit their website: http://www. dol. gov/compliance/laws/comp-vevraa. htm

4. Remedies
Back pay
Hiring
Promotion
Reinstatement
Termination of current federal contracts
Debarment from future federal contracts

R. Uniformed Services Employment and Reemployment Rights Act (USERRA)
1. Discrimination Prohibited
Employment discrimination based on military service or obligation

2. Coverage
Protects uniformed service members' reemployment rights when returning from a period of service, including those called up from the reserves or National Guard

3. Enforcement
Department of Labor (DOL), Veterans Employment and Training Service (VETS)
Call 1-866-487-2365, 1-202-693-4770, or 1-877-899-5627 (TTY).
Visit their website at www. dol. gov/vets

4. Remedies
Return to a job
Back pay
Lost Benefits
Corrected personnel files
Lost promotional opportunities
Retroactive seniority
Pension adjustments
Restored vacation

S. Genetic Information Nondiscrimination Act of 2008 (GINA)
1. Discrimination Prohibited
Genetic Discrimination and Protection of Genetic information

2. Coverage
Employers with fifteen or more employees

3. Enforcement Agency
Equal Employment Opportunity Commission (EEOC)
Contact the EEOC at 1-800-669-4000, visit their website at www. eeoc. gov, or contact a local office in your state.

4. Remedies
Compensatory damages
Punitive damages
Back pay and interest
Hiring
Promotion
Affirmative Action

APPENDIX D:
State Fair Employment Agencies

(See Glossary of Terms, Appendix A,
for definition of TTY, Text Telephone, and TDD,
Telephone Communication Device for the Deaf.)

Alabama Department of Human Resources, Equal Employment and Civil Rights Division
50 N. Ripley Street
Montgomery, AL 36130
Phone: 334-242-1550
Fax: 334-353-1491
TDD: 334-242-0196
Website: http://www.dhr.state.al.us/Index.asp

Alaska Human Rights Commission
800 A Street, Suite 204, Anchorage, AK 99501
Phone: 907-274-4692
TTY/TDD: 907-276-3177
Website: http://gov.state.ak.us/aschr

Arizona State Attorney General, Civil Rights Division
402 W. Congress South Bldg. #215
Tucson, AZ 85701
Phone Tucson: 520-628-6500
TDD: 520-628-6872
Phone Phoenix: 602-541-5263
TDD: 602-542-5002
Website: www.attorney-general.state.az.us/civil_rights

Arkansas is one of two states that does not have a State Fair Employment Agency.
Claims should be filed through the EEOC.
EEOC Little Rock Area Office
820 Louisiana Street, Suite 200
Little Rock, AR 72201
Phone: 501- 324-5060
Fax: 501-324-5991

California Department of Fair Employment and Housing
2014 T Street, Suite 210
Sacramento, CA 95814
Phone: 916-227-2878
Website: www.dfeh.ca.gov
and
California Department of Justice Civil Rights Enforcement Section
Public Inquiry Unit, P. O. Box 944255
Sacramento, Ca. 94244-2550
Phone: 916-322-3360
Website: http://ag.ca.gov/civil.php

Colorado Civil Rights Division Commission
1560 Broadway, Suite 1050
Denver, CO 80202-5143
Phone: 303-894-2997
Fax: 303-894-7830
TDD: 303-894-7382
Website: www.dora.state.co.us/civil-rights/

Connecticut Human Rights Protection and Advocacy
(Connecticut Office of Protection and Advocacy and Connecticut Commission on Human Rights and Opportunities have consolidated.)
21 Grand Street, Room 400
Hartford, Ct. 06106
Phone: 860-541-3400
Fax: 860-246-5068
TDD: 860-541-3459
Website: http://www.ct.gov/chro/site/default.asp

Delaware Division of Human Relations
820 North French St., 8th floor
Wilmington, DE
Phone: 302-577-5050
Fax: 302-577-3486
Website: http://statehumanrelations.delaware.gov

District of Columbia
DC Office of Human Rights
441 4th St. , N. W. Suite 570
Washington DC 20001
Phone: 202-727-4559
Fax: 202-727-9589
TTY Relay: 711
Website: http://ohr.dc.gov/ohr/site/default.asp

Florida Commission on Human Relations
2009 Apalachee Parkway, Suite 100
Tallahassee, FL 32302
Phone: 850-488-7082
Fax: 850-488-5291
TDD: 800-955-1339
Statewide voice relay: 711
Website: http://fchr.state.fl.us

Georgia Commission on Equal Opportunity
2 Martin Luther King, Jr. Drive SE
Suite 1002, West Tower
Atlanta, Ga. 30334
Phone: 404-656-1736
1-800-473-OPEN
Fax: 404-656-4399
Website: http://www.gceo.state.ga.us

Hawaii Civil Rights Commission
830 Punchbowl St. , Room 411
Honolulu, HI 96813
Phone: 808-586-8636
Fax: 808-586-8655
TDD: 808-586-8692
Email: hcrc@aloha.net

Idaho Human Rights Commission *
317 W. Main St., 3rd Floor
P. O. Box 83720,
Boise, ID 83702
Phone: 208-334-2873
Fax; 208-334-2664
Tollfree: 888-249-7025
Website: humanrights.idaho.gov

Illinois Department of Human Rights
1000 West Randolph St., Suite 5-100
Chicago, Il 60601
Phone: 312-814-6269
Fax: 312-814-6517
TDD: 312-814-4760
Website: www.state.il.usa/dhr

Indiana Civil Rights Commission
Indiana Government Center North
100 North Senate, N103
Indianapolis, Indiana 46204
Phone: 317-2322600
Fax: 317-232-6580
TDD: 800-743-3333
Tollfree: 800-628-2909
Website: http://www.in.gov/icrc/

Iowa Civil Rights Commission
Grimes State Office Building
400 East 14th St., Room 201
Des Moines, IA 50319
Phone: 515-281-4121
Fax: 515-242-5840
Website: www.state.ia.us/government/crc

Kansas Human Rights Commission
900 Southwest Jackson, Suite 568-S
Topeka, KS 66612
Phone: 785-296-3206
Fax: 785-296-0589
Website: http://www.khrc.net

Kentucky Commission on Human Rights
The Heyburn Building, 7th Floor
322 West Broadway,
Louisville, KY 40202
Phone: 502-595-4024
Fax: 502-595-4801
TDD: 502-595-4084
Website: http://kchr.ky.gov

Louisiana Commission on Human Rights
1001 N. 23rd St., Room 268
Baton Rouge, Louisiana 70802
Phone: 225-342-6969
Fax: 225-342-2063
TDD: 1-888-248-0859
Website: http://www.gov.state.la.us/humanrights/humanrightshome.htm

Maine Human Rights Commission
State House, Station 51,
Augusta, ME 04333
Phone: 207-624-6290
Fax: 207-624-8729
TTY: Maine Relay 711
Website: http://www.state.me.us/mhrc

Maryland Commission on Human Relations
6 St. Paul St. , 9th Floor
William Schaefer Tower
Baltimore, MD 21202-1631
Phone: 410-767-8600
Fax: 410-333-1841
TTY: 410-333-1737
Website: www.mchr.state.md.us

Massachusetts Commission Against Discrimination
One Ashburton Place, Room 601
Boston, MA 02108
Phone: 617-994-6000
Fax: 617-994-6024
Website: http://www.mass. gov/mcad/

Michigan Department of Civil Rights
Capital Tower Building, Suite 800
110 W. Michigan Avenue
Lansing, MI 48933
Phone: 517-335-3165
Fax: 517-241-0546
TTY: 517-241-1985
Website: http://www.michigan.gov/mdcr

Minnesota Department of Human Rights
Army Corps of Engineers Center
190 E. 5th Street, Suite 700
St. Paul, MN 55101
Phone: 800-657-3704
Fax: 651-296-9042
TTY: 651-296-1283
Website: http://www.humanrights.state.mn.us.index.html

Mississippi is one of two states that does not have a State Fair Employment
Agency.
The Birmingham District EEOC Office has jurisdiction over Mississippi.
Birmingham District EEOC Office
Ridge Park Place
1130 22nd Street South, Ste. 2000
Birmingham, AL 35205

Missouri Commission on Human Rights*
3315 W. Truman Blvd., P. O. Box 1129
Jefferson City, MO 65102-1129
Phone: 573-751-3325
Fax: 573-526-5090
TDD: 573-340-7590
Website: http://www.labor.mo.gov/mohumanrights

Montana Human Rights Bureau *
1625 11 Avenue, P. O. Box 1728
Helena, MT 59624
Phone: 406-444-2884
Fax: 406-444-2798
Website: http://erd.dli.mt.gov/humanright/hrhome.asp

Nebraska Equal Opportunity Commission
301 Centennial Mall South, Fifth Floor
P. O. Box 94934, Lincoln, NE 68508
Phone: 402-471-2024
Fax: 402-471-4059
Website: http://www.neoc.ne.gov

Nevada Equal Rights Commission
1820 East Sahara Ave., Suite 314
Las Vegas, NV 89104
Phone: 702-486-7161
Fax: 702-486-7054
Nevada Relay 711 or 800-326-6868
Website: http://detr.state.nv.us/nerc.htm

New Hampshire Commission on Human Rights
2 Chenell Drive
Concord, NH 03301-6053
Phone: 603-271-2767
Fax: 603-271-6339
TDD: 800-735-2964
E-mail: humanrights@nhsa.state.nh.us

New Jersey Division on Civil Rights
CN089, 140 E. Front St. , 6th floor
P. O. Box 089, Trenton, NJ 08625-0089
Phone: 609-292-4605
Fax: 609-984-3812
TTY: 609-292-1785
Website: http://www.nj.gov.oag.dcr.commission.html

New Mexico* Human Rights Bureau
1596 Pacheco St., Suite 103
Santa Fe, NM 87505
Phone: 505-827-6838 or 1-800-566-9471
Website: http://www.dhr.state.ny.us

New York State Division of Human Rights
One Fordham Plaza, 4th floor
Bronx, New York, 10458
Phone: 718-741-8400 or 1-888-392-3644
Website: www.DHR.NY.Gov

North Carolina Human Relations Commission
116 West Jones Street, Suite 2109
Raleigh, NC 27601
Phone: 919-807-4420
Fax: 919-807-4435
TDD: 919-733-7996
Website: http://www.doa.state.nc.us/hrc

North Dakota Department of Labor
600 East Boulevard, Department 406
Bismarck, ND 58505-0340
Phone: 701-328-2660
Fax: 701-328-2031
Website: www.nd.gov/labor/services/human-rights

Ohio Civil Rights Commission
State Office Tower, 30 East Broad Street, Fifth Floor
Columbus, OH 43215-3414
Phone: 614-466-2785
Fax: 614-466-7742
TDD: 614-469-9353
Website: http://crc.ohio.gov

Oklahoma Human Rights Commission
(Ceased operation June 30, 2012 and duties assumed by the Attorney General)
313 NE 21st St.,
Oklahoma City, Ok 73105
Phone: 405-521-3921
Website: http://www.ok.gov/ohrc/

Oregon Civil Rights Division, Bureau of Labor and Industries*
800 NE Oregon St. , Suite 1045
Portland, OR 97232
Phone: 971-673-0764
Fax: 971-673-0765
Website: http:///www.oregon.gov/BOLI/CRD/contact.us.html

Pennsylvania Human Relations Commission
301 Chestnut Street, Suite 300
Harrisburg, PA 17101-2702
Phone: 717-786-4412
Fax: 717-786-0420
TDD: 717-783-9308
Website: http://www.phrc.state.pa

Rhode Island Commission for Human Rights
180 Westminster Street, 3rd Floor
Providence RI 02903
Phone: 401-222-2661
Fax: 401-222-2616
TDD: 401-222-2664
Website: http://richr.state.us.frames.html

South Carolina Human Affairs Commission
2611 Forest Drive, Suite 200
Columbia, SC 29240
Phone: 803-737-7800
Fax; 803-253-4191
TDD: 803-253-4125
Website: http://www.state.sc.us.schac

South Dakota Division Human Rights, South Dakota Department of Labor*
700 Governors Drive, Kneip Building
Pierre, SD 57501
Phone: 605-773-3681
Fax: 605-733-4211
Website: http://dol.sd.gov/humanrights/default.aspx

Tennessee Human Rights Commission
710 James Robinson Parkway, Suite 100
Nashville, TN 37243-1219
Phone: 615-741-5825
Fax: 615:253-1886
Website: http://www.state.tn.us/humanrights

Texas Workforce Commission/Commission on Human Rights*
1117 Trinity Street, Suite 144 T
Austin, TX 78701-1919
Phone: 512-463-4678
Fax: 512-437-2643
Website: http://www.twc.state.tx.us/customers/semp/sempsubcrd.html

Utah Anti-Discrimination Division and Labor Division*
160 East 300 South, Third Floor
Salt Lake City, UT 84111
Phone: 801-530-6800
Fax: 801-530-6709
Website: http://laborcommission.utah.gov/Antidiscriminationandlabor/index.html

Vermont State Civil Rights Division, Office of Attorney General
State of Vermont
109 State Street, Pavilion Office Building
Montpelier, Vermont 05609-1001
Phone: 802-828-3657
Fax: 802-828-2154
TDD: 802-828-3665
Website: http://www.atg.state.vt.us/issues/employment-law.php

Commonwealth of Virginia Council on Human Rights*
(Merged with the Office of Attorney General)
1100 Bank Street, 12ᵗʰ Floor
Richmond, VA 23219
Phone: 804-225-2292 or 804-225-3294
Website: http://chr.vipnet.org

Washington State Human Rights Commission
711 S. Capitol Way, Suite 402
P. O. Box 42490
Olympia, WA 95804-2490
Phone: 360-753-6770
Fax: 360-586-2282
TDD: 800-300-7525
Website: http://www.hum.wa.gov

West Virginia Human Rights Commission
1321 Plaza East Room 108A
Charleston WV 25301-1400
Phone: 304-588-2616
Fax:304-588-0085
Website: http://www.wvf.state.wv.us.shrc

Wisconsin Department of Workforce Development, Equal Rights Division
201 E. Washington Avenue
Madison, WI 57308
Phone: 608-266-6860
Fax: 608-267-4592
TYY: 608-264-8752
Website: http://www.dwd.state.wi.us

Wyoming Department of Employment, Labor Standards Division
1510 East Pershing, West Wing, Room 150
Cheyenne, WY 82002
Phone: 307-777-7261
Fax: 307-777-5633
TDD: 307-777-7261
Website: http://doe.wyo.gov/Pages/default.aspx

*For economic reasons, these states have merged their human rights commissions with their state departments of labor or with their Office of Attorney General.

Author Page

Mary Greenwood is an attorney, human resources director, and author of the award-winning books *How to Negotiate Like a Pro* and *How to Mediate Like a Pro,* as well as *Hiring, Firing and Supervising Employees: An Employer's Guide to Discrimination Laws.* She has a BA and MA in English and a JD in Law and an LLM in Labor Law.

She has worked as head of human resources at Winter Park, Hollywood, Miami Beach, Monroe County, Keys Energy (Key West), and Roger Williams University. She has worked as legal counsel at Colorado College, University of North Carolina-Greensboro, Winthrop University, Manatee County, and Monroe County. She has taught Labor Law, Discrimination Law and Education Law at St. Thomas Law School, Stetson Law School, Troy State, Winthrop University, St. Leo's College and Barry Law School. She is a mediator, arbitrator and negotiator. At last count, she has had at least twenty-four jobs and wishes she had had this book available at some of her interviews. She lives in the Orlando area with her Boston Terrier, Annabelle.

How to Interview Like a Pro has won twelve book awards and is designated Star, Readers Choice and Editor's Choice by iUniverse.
1. Winner, Indie Excellence Awards, Career
2. Winner, Reader Views Literary Book Awards, How To
3. Winner, Silver Award, ForeWord Book Awards, Career
4. Winner, Pinnacle Book Achievement Awards, Business
5. Finalist, International Book Awards, Career
6. Finalist, Eric Hoffer Book awards
7. Finalist, Next Generation Indie Book Awards, Career
8. Finalist, USA Book Awards, Business/Finance
9. Honorable Mention, Readers Favorite, Business

10. Honorable Mention, DIY Book Awards, How To
11. Honorable Mention, New York Book Festival, How To
12. Extra Mention, Millenium Publishing Book Awards

How to Negotiate Like a Pro has won nine book awards
1. Second Edition,Winner, Indie Excellence Awards, Self-Help
2. Second Edition, Finalist, International Book Awards, Business
3. Winner, DIY Book festival, How To
4. Finalist, USA Book News, Self-Help
5. Finalist, ForeWord Book of the Year Awards, Self-Help
6. Runner-Up, New York Book Festival, Self-Help
7. Runner-Up, New York Book Festival, E-Book
8. Honorable Mention, London Book Festival, Self-Help
9. Finalist, Readers Favorite Book Awards, Self-Help

How to Mediate Like a Pro has won twelve book awards.
1. Winner, USA Book News, Law
2. Winner , Indie Excellence Awards, E-book
3. Winner, Readers View Book Awards, How To
4. Winner, Beach Book Festival, How To
5. Winner, New York Book Festival, E-Book
6. Winner, Pinnacle Book Achievement Awards
7. Winner, Silver Prize, ForeWord, Book of the Year Awards, Self-Help
8. Spirit Award, South Florida Writers Association
9. Finalist, Next Generation Indie Books, Business,
10. Runner-Up. New England Book Festival, How To
11. Honorable Mention. London Book Festival, How To
12. Runner-Up, DIY Book Festival, E-Book

How to Mediate Like a Pro and *How to Negotiate Like a Pro* have been published in Kenya and India.

If you have an interesting interview story, a good interview question or want to contact Mary, her email address is Howtointerview@aol.com. Website: http://www.howtointerviewlikeapro.org
and http://www.marygreenwood.org

CPSIA information can be obtained at www.ICGtesting.com
Printed in the USA
LVOW101618280113

317566LV00017B/867/P

9 781938 908064